THE COMPASS WITHIN

THE COMPASS WITHIN

Guiding Life with Perspective

Gabriel Davis

Dedicated to my mother, on her special day. Releasing this book on your birthday feels like the perfect way to honor you. I am so grateful for you and all the love and support you have given me. I love you.

About the Author

Gabriel Davis published his first book at the age of twenty-one, marking the beginning of a journey defined by relentless curiosity, a growth mindset, and continuous improvement. As a Presidential Scholar and the only student in his grade to pursue and be accepted into a prestigious double-degree program between the University of San Diego and a partner institution in Rome, Italy, Gabriel exemplifies a polymathic approach to life, seamlessly integrating diverse interests and skills into a unified vision of success.

As an avid athlete, he uses sports to build discipline and push personal boundaries. His travels to over eighty countries have enriched his perspective, fueling a deep appreciation for culture, adaptability, and life itself.

Passionate about leadership and entrepreneurship, Gabriel continually seeks to grow, provide value, and create opportunities for others. Anchored by a wonderful family that has supported and shaped his path, Gabriel is committed to becoming the best version of himself while inspiring those around him to do the same.

Readers can connect with Gabriel at
linkedin.com/in/gabrieldavis03

Book design by Adam Hay Studio, UK
Illiustrations by @lukasz.ziabka.

ISBN: 979-8-218-60497-4
LCCN: 2025901817

Printed in the United States of America

Contents

Introduction

I began *The Compass Within* at age nineteen and completed it at age twenty-one. With the full picture now in sight, I see this book as a testament to the transformative power of *curiosity* and *resilience*. Each page documents ideas that have contributed to my growth and understanding, with the aim of sharing these insights so they may provide meaningful value to others, not just to myself. I also detail the significance of our inner compass and perspective as tools anyone can develop to navigate life's challenges.

I hope to show that impact is not always about age but rather about exposure, awareness, and an eagerness to learn. Growing up in a world dominated by technology, we have seen firsthand the effects of social media: how it can fuel cheap dopamine hits, endless scrolling, and surface-level connections. Consciously engaging with content that nurtures learning and self-growth, I've come to see that if you want to gain fluency in a particular language—whether it's a literal language, a field of study, or a skill—you must surround yourself with those who speak that language. This applies universally. Falling in love with learning concepts that have a real-world impact, such as perspective and mindset, has shaped my ambition, goals, and resilience.

As children, many of us hold dreams we perceive as "big"—owning a sports car, becoming a pro-athlete, or living in a million-dollar home. But as life unfolds, new layers of reality emerge, and our dreams change. We gain ambition for new goals that feel rewarding and possible, while letting go of others that no longer resonate. For me, this one phrase keeps my dreams alive: "What if I am thinking too small?" This question rekindles my optimism and fuels my long-term goals, reminding me to keep pushing the boundaries of what I believe is possible. At age eighteen, I would have struggled to believe that I'd publish a book by age twenty-one, yet here I am—proof that as our knowledge and experiences grow, so does our sense of what we can achieve.

In a world that often values experience based solely on age, this book aims to show that clarity, adaptability, and purpose aren't limited by years, but can be achieved through intentional growth. I challenge readers of all ages to view life through a lens of continual growth and discovery. Ultimately, this book is meant to encourage you to push beyond comfort zones, find strength in struggle, and unlock new possibilities within yourself by aligning with your inner compass and seeking a new perspective—at any stage of life you are in.

On January 3, 2023, I conceived my first detailed business plan, which set off a powerful upward spiral of learning. Diving headfirst into entrepreneurship, I realized that success in the business world, and in life, often comes down to mindset and perspective. Or as my dad would say, "It's all between the ears." I later realized its impact on daily life as well. As I researched various startups—from real estate and clothing brands to ATM machines and trading—I noticed a recurring theme: the entrepreneurs who excelled all shared a specific mental framework that allowed them to thrive. I will share their perspectives throughout each chapter.

This book is my way of documenting that journey—much like a personal journal—with the goal of helping others tap into the same principles of perspective that I discovered along the way. I believe that what is learned must be shared. Knowledge gains value when passed on, and it would feel limiting to keep these lessons to myself when they could be used to help others. By writing this book, I hope to provide others with the tools to grow and have them benefit from the wisdom I've encountered.

Growing up, travel was a constant in my life, allowing me to experience new cultures, environments, and philosophies. Gratefully, by the age of twenty-one, I had visited over eighty countries, which shaped my worldview in ways that would have been impossible otherwise. Every place I visited offered a new lesson—whether it was through architecture, the way people interacted, or the strategies they employed in their daily lives. I came to realize that every culture has something to teach us, and the more I learned, the more I grew.

I'm a polymath—a curious explorer of life, embracing lifelong learning and constantly pushing the boundaries of personal growth. Exposure to different cultures, sports, languages, and philosophies has broadened my ability to relate to others. I've experienced a multitude of perspectives, which have allowed me to find value in a diverse range of ideas and experiences. My journey includes challenges and goals, such as completing a double degree program; graduating law school; learning conversational Italian; training in jiu jitsu, muay thai, and boxing; running half marathons; and owning multiple firms. Having immersed myself in different perspectives across the world, I fuel my passion for developing diverse skills and striving for growth. Anchored by *faith*, *family*, and *freedom*, I believe that through adversity comes strength. Each day, I aim to embrace challenges as opportunities to learn and evolve, knowing that every experience adds depth and resilience to my journey.

We each have a compass within that serves as our internal guidance system, helping us align with our authentic self, values, and purpose. This inner compass also plays a crucial role in stregthening self-awareness, decision-making, and intentional living. When we are aware of our feelings and motivations, we can make decisions that are more aligned with our true selves. This compass guides us in making decisions that feel "right" at a deeper level. Often this involves listening to our gut feelings or intuition, which are reflections of our inner wisdom. In that same vein, the power of perspective is an ally with our inner compass as it shapes how we experience the world, approach challenges, and make decisions. Perspective determines whether we see obstacles as roadblocks or opportunities, whether we view failures as defeats or lessons. It is the lens through which we interpret events, relationships, and our own potential.

Before you tap into your inner compass and map out the areas where you need a shift in perspective, let me offer a word of advice: *You can't change people directly; you can only help them change the way people perceive them.* This book is about *you* and what you can do to initiate changes *within*. If you blame others for your shortcomings, or complain about how no one believes in you, or allow yourself to be dragged down by the negativity of others, then your inner compass is off-track. Self-responsibility means being accountable for yourself and how you live and interact with others. When you are able to pause, gain perspective, and realign your path, your life elevates, which then has the power to elevate others too. Perspective is what separates those who stagnate from those who succeed, in every definition of the word, and it's something we can all cultivate. Whether it's learning from failures, navigating the complexities of relationships, or maintaining discipline in the face of adversity, my goal is to help you unlock new doors that hold opportunities you may not have known existed.

The mistake most people make is that they are looking for *what to do* instead of who to become. *Becoming* over *doing* is what will set you apart from those who are caught up in an exhausted loop of people-pleasing, striving, and limiting beliefs. Living with intention and understanding the power of perspective will drastically alter your life's course. To help you understand how significant a shift in your mindset can be, I will be focusing on successful people who understand these truths about perspective.

The choice before you is simple. You get back the energy you put forth. You can choose to have a negative perspective, which will guarantee negative results. Or you can choose to have a perspective that is fueled by optimism, hopefulness, and solution-based scenarios, which will eventually manifest in your life as freedom, inner peace, and success. This book offers the key to adaptability, resilience, and continuous growth. It encourages you to be 1 percent better every day, to stay grounded in solid personal philosophies, to love learning, and to take consistent action. It highlights the importance of surrounding yourself with the right people, focusing on small wins, and building a mindset that is immune to outside distractions without reason.

When engaging with this book, I encourage you to maintain an open mind. The aim is not for you to adopt every idea presented, but to challenge your own beliefs and broaden your understanding. By exposing yourself to different viewpoints and philosophies, you will have the opportunity to enhance and evolve your own perspective. Approach each chapter with curiosity and reflection, allowing the stories and insights to guide you in building a more well-rounded and adaptable mindset.

I suggest taking time to reflect on each chapter. Highlight the sections that resonate with you, and make note of the stories or ideas you find interesting. Whether you choose to focus on an entire chapter or just a particular concept, use this book as a guide to inform your own journey of growth and self-improvement. Consistently practicing the principles within these pages will help you tap into your compass within, shift your perspective, and develop the mental frameworks that are necessary for success, fulfillment, and a balanced life.

1
Pairing the Compass Within with Perspective

Perspective is the lens through which we view and interpret the world around us. It shapes how we understand life events, people, and situations, guiding our responses and influencing our thoughts, feelings, and actions. Perspective is not about controlling every thought but choosing which ones to focus on, enabling us to break free from limiting beliefs, embrace paradoxes, and reframe challenges as opportunities for growth. It provides clarity, empowering us to make purposeful decisions and align our actions with our values and goals. Through perspective, we gain mastery over our mindset, emotional resilience, and creativity, transforming life's obstacles into opportunities for personal evolution. Ultimately, perspective is the key to defining our reality and creating a life of meaning and fulfillment. In a nutshell, *perspective is the lens through which we shape our reality, guiding every thought, action, and outcome.*

Thoughts are like waves in the ocean. You can't stop them from coming, but you can choose which ones to ride. Our perspective shapes this choice. If we focus on negative, fearful, or self-limiting thoughts, we ride waves that take us into turbulent waters. But if we consciously choose to surf thoughts of positivity, growth, and possibility, we chart a course toward fulfillment and success. What we focus on shapes how we feel, and how we feel determines what we do. Ultimately, what we do becomes who we are. Perspective, then, is the ability to select which waves of thought to ride, knowing that the thoughts we choose to dwell on define our reality.

Many people are so trapped in their minds that they don't even realize it. We create mental prisons, walls built from limiting beliefs, fears, and habitual thought patterns. The first step toward freedom is recognizing that you're imprisoned. If you believe you're already free, you won't try to escape. This concept touches the core of self-awareness. When we're oblivious to the invisible chains that bind us—whether it's our insecurities, negative self-talk, or the stories we tell ourselves—we remain stuck.

Escaping this mental prison requires a deep understanding of the barriers you've constructed. Once you acknowledge them, only then can you dismantle these walls. The key to freedom lies in self-awareness and the willingness to confront the uncomfortable truth that you're often the architect of your own confinement.

Mastering Your Mind Is the Key to Control

Learning to select your thoughts is like selecting your clothes each day. This analogy highlights that thought control is not automatic; it's a skill that must be cultivated. Many of us struggle because we spend so much time trying to control external circumstances, yet the only thing we truly have control over is our mind. If we can't master our thoughts, we will always be enslaved by them.

Perspective teaches us that surrendering control of everything but our mind is the path to true freedom. The more we try to control the uncontrollable, the more frustrated and anxious we become. Instead, focus on controlling your response to what life throws at you. It's not about "trying" to stop thinking or trying too hard to control; it's about letting go, quieting the mind, and allowing peace to emerge naturally. As the saying goes, "Stop trying, and start surrendering," and in that quiet space, you'll find clarity.

> *"When you change the way you look at things, the things you look at change."* —Wayne Dyer

The Greek philosopher Plato offers a timeless allegory in "The Cave," where prisoners mistake shadows for reality. This allegory reminds us that, like the cave's prisoners, we can easily fall into a habit of accepting illusions—societal expectations, limiting beliefs, and unchallenged ideas—as the truth. Just as the cave dwellers mistake shadows for reality, we often base our perceptions on incomplete or distorted information. Plato's message is simple yet profound: without questioning our views and assumptions, we may remain stuck in darkness, mistaking illusions for truth.[1]

In life, many of our pursuits—such as the allure of fame, ideal relationships, or prestigious careers—are less tangible than we believe. These desires are often illusions projected by society, shaping what we think we should value. As a result, we chase goals that may not even be our own, losing touch with what truly matters. Understanding this allegory emphasizes why "the unexamined life is not worth living," as Socrates famously said.[2] Escaping the cave means gaining the courage to question

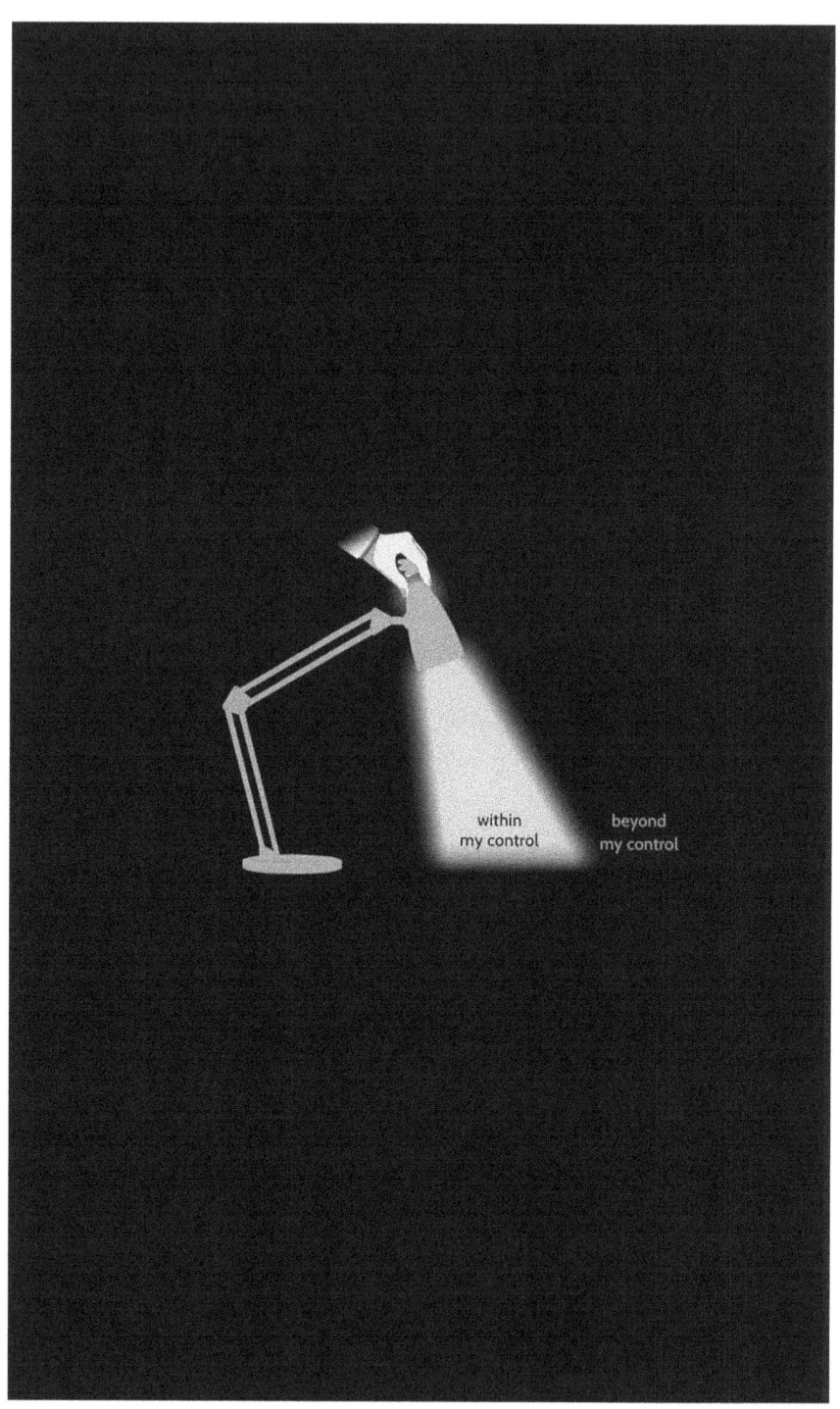

within
my control

beyond
my control

our beliefs, to see beyond mere shadows, and to seek true knowledge. It's a call to enlightenment that challenges us to leave behind comfort and familiar delusions, seeking clarity in a world often clouded by illusions.

Plato's cave urges us to illuminate our perspectives, urging us to ask: Will we have the courage to journey toward enlightenment, even if it requires distancing ourselves from familiar views? Or will we remain nestled in the comfort of familiar delusions? As philosopher and mystic Manly P. Hall wisely noted, "The hours may be long, and the teachers cruel, but each of us must walk that path."[3] This journey is the essence of perspective—an invitation to question, discover, and redefine reality on our own terms.

Setting the Course: The Power of Clear Direction

Entrepreneur Luke Belmar offers a powerful analogy to illustrate the importance of clarity and direction. Imagine we're standing on the top deck of a yacht, up at the captain's station. If I told the captain, "I want to go from Miami to a specific port in Jamaica," he wouldn't hesitate. Within seconds, he'd be able to tell me the exact route, the distance, and even the estimated time of arrival. He understands the journey because he knows precisely where he's headed. Even though he can't yet see Jamaica, he follows each step with confidence, knowing that if he stays on course, he will eventually arrive.[4]

The same principle applies to our personal and professional journeys. Once you're clear on your destination, the path becomes much less confusing. It's no longer a vague or dark process, but rather a series of clear steps. You don't have to reinvent the wheel. Millions have succeeded before us. So instead of searching for some elusive secret, look at what others have done to achieve their goals. Identify the patterns, simplify the process, and model the behaviors and strategies that have already proven effective. Success lies in recognizing these patterns and optimizing them. You don't need to be special or unique to succeed—just focused, clear, and disciplined in following the steps to get where you want to go.

have a clear target   to hit your goal

The Compass Within

Embrace the Power of Paradox

Life operates by three essential rules: paradox, humor, and change. Paradox teaches us that life is full of contradictions—situations where we are both in control and yet confronted by the mystery of the unknown. The lesson here is not to waste time trying to figure everything out. Life is a paradox, and trying to make sense of every twist and turn will only drain us. The key is to accept the paradox and focus on what we can influence.

Perspective helps us manage this uncertainty. Instead of obsessing over outcomes, we learn to laugh at life's unpredictability, finding strength in humor. Humor allows us to lighten the load and navigate through difficulties with grace. Change reminds us that nothing stays the same. Life is in a constant state of flux, and our perspective must adapt to this reality. Embracing change rather than resisting it frees us to move forward. Perspective shifts from seeking control to embracing flow.

The idea of trust is often misunderstood, and its paradox reveals a deep truth about how we experience life. When you say, "I don't trust . . ." you are actually trusting in the belief that you lack it. This highlights the duality of experience. You can feel out of control, but at the same time, you are controlling that feeling. You can believe you are not confident, but in believing so, you're showing confidence in that belief.

This paradox reminds us that our feelings of lack or insecurity are, in themselves, a form of certainty. You are creating an experience where trust exists, even if it's in the negative form. If you can trust in your lack of trust, why can't you trust in your ability to have trust? The universe, as the analogy goes, doesn't care either way; it simply supports the energy you put out. This is where perspective becomes so crucial. When you shift your perception from a position of lack to one of possibility, you begin to realize that trust and confidence are choices you can lean into, just like their opposites.

This reframing of trust is empowering. You are no longer a passive victim of your circumstances. Instead, you are actively participating in the story you're telling yourself. The paradox allows you to see that whether you choose to trust in the positive or the negative, the universe will support that decision. The difference lies in the outcomes you want to experience. By tuning in to the compass within and shifting your trust toward what empowers you, you gain control over your narrative and your life.

Entrepreneur Derik Fay shares an inspiring story about a little boy born with one arm who learned judo. Despite his physical limitations, his sensei agreed to train him, but for two years the boy was only taught a single move. Understandably, the boy felt afraid and unsure when he entered his first judo tournament. He only knew one move, and his opponents had both arms and a wider array of skills. However, to his surprise, he easily defeated every opponent, including in the final match. When he asked his sensei how he had won with just one move, the sensei explained that the only defense against the move required grabbing the opponent's left arm—something his opponents couldn't do.[5]

The boy's greatest perceived weakness—his missing arm—was transformed into his greatest strength. Instead of focusing on everything he couldn't do, he leaned into what he could do, mastering one thing to the point where it became unbeatable. This shift in perspective teaches us that we don't have to be good at everything. In fact, we can be bad at many things, but if we find one thing we excel at, it can become a game-changer.

Often, the thing we view as our limitation or flaw is the very thing that holds the key to our success. We spend so much time trying to hide or fix what we believe makes us broken, but sometimes, leaning into that perceived weakness reveals an incredible strength. Perspective transforms how we see our limitations, turning what might initially seem like a disadvantage into an unparalleled advantage.

This concept isn't just about judo; it's about life. We all have areas where we feel less capable or where we struggle. But instead of fixating on what we can't do, shifting our focus to what we can do—and doing it well—can lead to unexpected victories. When we embrace our unique qualities, no matter how unconventional they may seem, we unlock a strength that allows us to soar, often in ways we never imagined.

Shift Your Perspective on Wealth

Finance author Morgan Housel offers a profound redefinition of wealth: "The best measure of wealth is what you have minus what you want, and by this measure, some billionaires are broke."[6] This perspective shift is powerful because it reframes wealth not as a matter of accumulation, but as a balance between desires and reality. Someone who has everything but still wants more is, in effect, living in a state of poverty, perpetually chasing something that remains exclusive.

It's not about how much you can collect, but how content you are with what you already possess. When you want less, you inherently have more. Billionaires who constantly strive for more are, in a way, poorer than those who find peace in contentment. This shift reminds us that wealth isn't only external; it's internal, rooted in gratitude and perspective. *The wealthiest people, then, are those who have mastered the art of wanting less.*

Analogy of the Pencil

Just like a pencil, you need regular "sharpening" to remain effective. The process of sharpening, while painful, is necessary for growth. It represents the struggles, challenges, and obstacles we face, which build character and refine us. Without these hardships, we remain dull and ineffective. It's through adversity that we sharpen our skills, learn resilience, and become better versions of ourselves. Mistakes are inevitable, but they are not permanent. Like the pencil's eraser, we have the ability to correct our errors. Mistakes are not failures if we learn from them. They are lessons in disguise, providing opportunities for improvement. Life is not about avoiding mistakes; it's about growing through them.

We leave our mark everywhere we go. Every action, every word contributes to our personal story. Every difficulty becomes a stepping stone if we shift our perspective. Each moment of life is another chapter in our narrative, and it's up to us to keep writing it with purpose and integrity. Remember, the most important part of the pencil, and of ourselves, is what's inside. Our inner strength, character, and values define who we are, much more than external circumstances. By recognizing that what matters most is internal, we free ourselves from the pressure of external validation and societal expectations. This is where perspective becomes transformative—it allows us to focus on growth from within, knowing that the outside world will reflect our internal state.

Emotional Intelligence: Gaining Control Over Your Reactions

If you can be in a bad mood for no reason, you can also choose to be in a good mood for no reason. Mood is often a choice. Break free from the belief that external circumstances must dictate our emotional state. Many people live in emotional reactivity, believing that things need to go well for them to feel good. But this thought pattern traps you in a cycle where your peace of mind is at the mercy of life's unpredictable events.

- Once you understand the power of your words,
  you won't just say anything.

- Once you understand the power of your thoughts,
  you won't just think anything.

- Once you understand the power of your presence,
  you won't just be anywhere.

- Once you understand the power of your actions,
  you won't just do anything.

- Once you understand the power of your relationships,
  you won't just associate with anyone.

- Once you understand the power of your energy,
  you won't waste it on negativity.

- Once you understand the power of your attention,
  you won't just give it to anything.

- Once you understand the power of your beliefs,
  you won't just believe anything.

You don't have to buy into the emotional cost of a bad day. If something doesn't impact your long-term well-being, why should it ruin your peace? This awareness frees you to reclaim control over your mood, realizing that you can have a great day regardless of external conditions. Emotional resilience, then, becomes about choosing how to feel and not letting outside factors dictate your internal state.

The phrase, "If someone can make you mad, they can control you," is a powerful reminder of the importance of emotional intelligence. Emotions, when unchecked, can become tools for manipulation—both by external forces and by our own internal struggles. Learning to master your emotions is essential for navigating life with clarity and strength. Emotional intelligence (EQ) is about recognizing, understanding, and managing your emotions so that you are not easily swayed by outside influences. It's the ability to take deep breaths, to pause before reacting, and to not allow someone else's actions to pull you out of character. This level of control is a crucial aspect of perspective because it allows you to step back from the immediacy of the emotion and evaluate the situation with a clear mind.

> *"Life is 10% what happens to us and 90% how we react to it." —Charles R. Swindoll*

The book *Emotional Intelligence* by Daniel Goleman encapsulates this idea, noting that while IQ (intellectual quotient) is important, EQ often plays a more critical role in success. In fact, many millionaires don't have the highest IQs, but they excel in EQ. They've mastered the ability to remain calm under pressure, to manage stress, and to navigate social interactions with poise.[7] In life, intelligence alone doesn't dictate success; your ability to handle emotional challenges does.

Keeping Promises to Yourself

If you continually break promises to yourself—whether it's hitting snooze after you promised to wake up early or skipping a workout you committed to—you start to lose self-respect. Perspective shows us that self-respect and self-esteem are built on trust in your own word. When you consistently follow through on the promises you make to yourself, no matter how small, you start to trust yourself more. Over time, these small actions compound, and your self-respect grows.

It's not about grand gestures or huge leaps forward—it's about doing the little things, like waking up on time or staying off your phone in the morning. These seemingly minor actions contribute to a broader sense of accomplishment and trust in yourself. The more you honor your word, the more you believe in your ability to achieve larger, more extraordinary goals. One of the fundamental challenges in life is that our brain is wired to avoid effort and seek comfort. However, there's a mental "hack" that radically changes this dynamic. Contrary to what many believe, the brain finds anticipation more rewarding than attainment. The satisfaction we experience doesn't come from reaching a goal but from the process

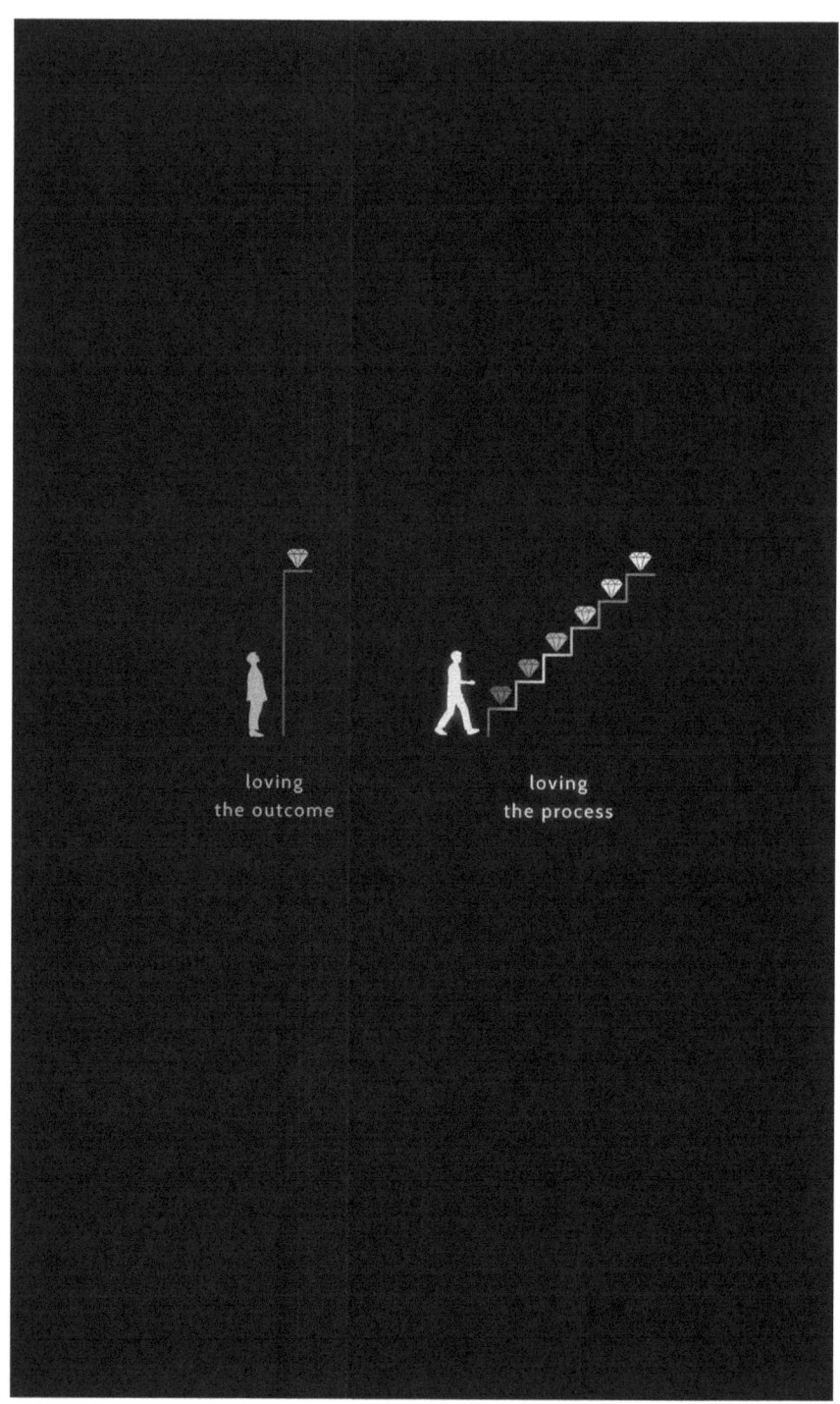

loving
the outcome

loving
the process

of getting there. Once your brain understands that a win follows effort, it begins to activate the reward system, and suddenly the process itself becomes enjoyable.

Instead of dreading hard work, you can train your mind to find joy in the process. Each step you take toward your goal becomes a win in itself, creating a cycle of positive reinforcement. It's no longer about enduring the hard times just to get to the reward; the journey becomes the reward. This change in mindset allows you to view challenges as opportunities, rewiring your brain to enjoy effort and perseverance.

Everything in life is a skill: discipline, patience, compassion. These aren't traits people are simply born with or without; they are cultivated through repetition and practice. When you realize that every aspect of life is a skill you can improve, it shatters the illusion that you're incapable of growth in certain areas. This perspective is liberating because it means you're no longer bound by limitations. If you struggle with discipline, you can train yourself to be disciplined through consistent practice. If you lack patience, you can develop it through repeated effort. The key is recognizing that success in any area comes from intentional, sustained practice. By changing how you view skills—from fixed attributes to something you can build—you unlock limitless potential. You no longer have an excuse to not pursue anything, knowing that with time and effort, you can become good at anything.

The Creativity Study

In a NASA study led by George Land and Beth Jarman in the 1960s, the term "genius" was defined by a person's ability to engage in divergent thinking, which is a key component of creativity. Divergent thinking refers to the ability to generate multiple solutions to a problem, rather than just one correct answer. It is the kind of thinking that leads to innovation, creativity, and problem-solving—characteristics that are often associated with genius-level creativity.

The study tested 1,600 five year olds for divergent thinking, a measure of creativity, and found that 98 percent of them scored at the "genius" level. However, as the children grew older, the results showed a stark decline: by age ten, only 30 percent still qualified as geniuses, and by age fifteen, that number had dropped to just 12 percent. When the same test was administered to 280,000 adults (average age of thirty-one), only 2 percent retained their creative genius.[8] This dramatic decrease in creativity was largely attributed to formal education, which tends to suppress creativity in favor of more rigid, convergent thinking models. This study highlights an important shift in perspective: creativity is not something that naturally diminishes as we age. It is repressed by learned behaviors and systems that emphasize conformity over imagination.

The concept of *tabula rasa*—the idea that the mind is a blank slate at birth—suggests that our experiences shape the way we think. As we grow and encounter societal structures, such as traditional schooling, our natural creative instincts are often constrained by rules and expectations. However, just as uncreative behaviors are learned, creative behaviors can be relearned and cultivated. By shifting our perspective on creativity, we come to understand that we are not bound by a loss of imagination. We can reclaim our creative genius by cultivating curiosity, engaging in imaginative thinking, and breaking free from rigid thought patterns. Creativity, then, is not a rare talent but a skill that can be revived and enhanced through conscious effort and an open mind.

Create a Path to Your Goals

Jordan Peterson emphasizes the importance of having a clear vision and then moving toward it deliberately. "You can have what you want in five years, but two conditions must be met: You need to know what it is, and you have to aim at it."[9] Without knowing exactly what you want, there's no target to aim for, and without taking actionable steps, a vision remains just a dream.

Peterson highlights that clarity and intention are crucial when setting goals in any area of life: family, relationships, career, or personal well-being. When you define your goal, you immediately begin to direct your energy toward it. Writing it down and identifying specific actions creates momentum. Even the smallest movement toward that goal generates a sense of accomplishment, reinforcing the positive cycle of progress.

The pleasure lies in the *movement* toward your goal. This reframes success as not just reaching a destination, but finding satisfaction in each small step along the way. It's about continuously moving closer to something meaningful, rather than waiting for happiness at the finish line.

Perspective allows you to appreciate the journey, recognizing that growth happens in the pursuit, not just the achievement.

Author and motivational speaker Jim Rohn describes a direct challenge to your self-perception and potential. He frames success as not only possible but personal, asking, "Why not you?" This isn't a rhetorical question. It's a call to take control of your life and recognize your own ability to make significant changes. Rohn lists several empowering affirmations that outline what is possible if you decide to take action:

- **You've got the brains.**
  You are intelligent and capable of making decisions
  that will shape your future.

- **You can study the plan.**
  The resources and knowledge to succeed are available—
  you just need to engage with them.

- **You can change your life.**
  Your life doesn't have to stay the same. You have the
  power to grow, adapt, and evolve over time.

- **You can grow immensely in the next few years.**
  Change doesn't happen overnight, but consistent growth
  over time leads to profound transformation.

- **You can make your dreams come true.**
  With a clear vision and steady action, even the loftiest
  dreams are attainable.

- **You can build a financial wall around your family.**
  You can achieve financial stability and protect your
  loved ones by taking control of your financial future.

- **You can become healthy.**
  Physical well-being is within your reach through daily
  actions that contribute to better health.

- **You can become powerful.**
  Power comes from self-mastery, and the ability to
  influence your own life and, in turn, impact the world
  around you.[10]

The essence of Rohn's message is rooted in personal responsibility and empowerment. It's a shift in perspective from passive observer to active participant in your life. By asking, "Why not you?" Rohn is challenging you to reject excuses and take ownership of your potential. *Perspective allows you to see that the barriers between you and your goals are often self-imposed*, and, by changing your mindset, you can begin to unlock your full potential.

Personal Evolution and the Laws of the Universe

If you're not evolving, you're stagnating, and anything that limits the power of your mind delays your growth. This concept ties into the universal laws: the Law of Attraction, the Law of Abundance, and Equivalent Exchange. These laws guide how we move through life. For instance, what you focus on expands, meaning controlling your thoughts is crucial to directing your life's trajectory.

The Law of Abundance reminds us that the world is full of infinite possibilities; scarcity is often just a mindset. Equivalent Exchange teaches us that everything has a cost: effort for reward, action for consequence. Ultimately, *if we can't control our mind, we are enslaved by it. Freeing the mind from limitation allows us to grow and evolve continuously.* The power of perspective lies in realizing that life is but a thought, and by controlling our thoughts, we can shape our reality.

The simple yet profound question—"Would you take $10 million if you couldn't wake up tomorrow?"—forces a perspective shift on the value of life. Most people, when asked, would say no. This reveals a powerful truth: Waking up tomorrow is worth more than $10 million. We often lose sight of the immense value of life itself, taking for granted the gift of waking up each day. This exercise teaches us to cultivate gratitude for the very act of being alive.

If waking up tomorrow is more valuable than millions of dollars, how should that impact your daily perspective? It means that every day you wake up is a million-dollar opportunity. It's a reminder to approach each day with a smile, to carry the knowledge that your existence itself is a gift. The $10 million question also challenges you to prioritize peace of mind and purpose over material gain. It's a call to wake up every day with a sense of worth, knowing that the opportunity to live is priceless.

Patrick Bet-David, founder of Valuetainment, draws on an ancient Jewish proverb to highlight the importance of legacy. "Write a book, plant a tree, have a son."[11] These three acts are metaphors for creating something that outlives you, leaving a mark on the world. Whether through your words (the book), nurturing life (the tree), or raising a family (a son), the legacy you leave behind is a reflection of the value you bring to the world.

The message here is about perspective—thinking beyond your immediate life and considering how your actions today will echo for generations. Building a family or contributing to the world in a way that lasts is about creating something larger than yourself. By taking this long-term view, you align your daily actions with something greater than temporary success or fleeting pleasures. It's not just about accumulating wealth or achieving personal goals; it's about creating enduring impact, living a life that resonates long after you're gone.

2
Skillfully Navigating the Mountain

When climbing a mountain, preparation and strength are required, but descending a mountain requires precision and balance. When climbing your mountain, it is all about taking millions of small steps and setting little goals along the way: Take small breaks. Understand where you are and where you made it to. Recognize how far you have come. Evaluate which trail or path you should take next. Be aware of animals and other dangers. Realize who made it this far up with you and how many people started to fall behind. Be aware of what type of weather and adversities will set you back and make it more challenging. Ask yourself if you came well-prepared with the right skills, strength, and equipment needed to reach your desired height. Are you able to adapt in real-time to unseen events? Can you make the best decisions in terms of when to stop, drink, and refuel? Can you learn from the mistakes of carrying too much equipment on your back, not taking advantage of the supplies and tools you brought, or not utilizing your resources carefully and strategically?

There are so many little things along the journey, that we sometimes forget where we are because we sometimes focus on the summit more often than is beneficial. We should not fixate on the peak; instead, our focus should be on the next step in front of us. Keep moving, put one foot in front of the other, and before you know it, you will reach the top. Just as each of us climbers face unique challenges and experiences on the way to the summit, we encounter distinct trials and tribulations that are shaped by our perspectives. Recognizing that the path we follow or create, with its obstacles, is where the essence of life unfolds, allows us to find value and lessons in every experience. It's through this lens of perspective that the climb becomes a powerful metaphor for life, urging us to savor the moment, learn from the journey, and appreciate how our viewpoints shape our realities. In this way, the climb teaches us resilience, gratitude, and the significance of our attitudes as we navigate life's peaks and valleys.

"The journey of a thousand miles begins with a single step." —Lao Tzu

The Ascent: Preparation and Progress for the Journey

The ascent in both mountain climbing and the journey of life is influenced by the quality of preparation and the approach taken toward each step forward. This phase is not just about the physical act of moving upwards, but also about the mindset and strategic planning that precedes the climb. Emphasis on concentrating on immediate tasks rather than fixating on the distant summit serves as a crucial strategy for managing the many complexities of the challenges faced. This approach helps in breaking down the overwhelming goal of reaching the summit into manageable tasks, making the journey seem less daunting and more achievable.

Preparation includes a wide range of activities, from the physical conditioning required to endure the climb, to the specific selection of equipment that will support the journey. Just as climbers must assess and prepare for weather conditions, they must anticipate and plan for a multitude of conditions they might experience during the journey. Good preparation involves not only having the right tools and resources, but also setting an appropriate pace that aligns with the climber's capabilities and circumstances. This pace-setting is critical because it recognizes that success is not a race; it is a personal journey that allows for progress at a rate that is sustainable and aligned with one's strengths and limitations.

In addition, setting a pace early and adjusting it according to the conditions encountered reflects the importance of adaptability and self-awareness. Just as climbers must be mindful of the changing weather and adjust their pace to conserve energy, they must remain flexible in their goals and strategies, ready to modify their approach in response to the unpredictability of life. This adaptability enhances the chances of reaching the top of the mountain with minimal stress or obstacles.

The ascent of a mountain, much like the journey through life, is filled with unpredictability and challenges that are unique to each of our paths. As climbers, we might face sudden weather changes, from clear skies to a brewing storm, mirroring life's tendency to shift from calm to disruptive without warning. Injuries such as a rolled ankle or more severe accidents can occur unexpectedly, reflecting the physical and emotional setbacks we encounter in life. Physical limitations, whether from the inception or developed along the way, serve as a reminder of our individual boundaries and the need to adapt our strategies accordingly.

Similarly, external circumstances such as the availability of water

Everything is hard before it gets easy.

sources or the intensity of the sun's heat can drastically affect a climber's progress and comfort. These elements represent the external factors in life that we often have little control over, such as economic setbacks, societal changes, or unexpected personal setbacks. The unpredictability of these factors requires resilience and flexibility, qualities that are essential on both a mountain climb and life's journey.

The diversity of individual paths is shaped by various factors, including our outcome of the birth lottery, physical traits, and personal experiences. Just as two climbers may take different routes to the summit based on their strengths, preferences, and the challenges they face, so we navigate life's journey in ways that reflect our unique backgrounds and abilities. This variance highlights the importance of recognizing and respecting each person's journey, understanding that comparison can diminish the value of our own experiences.

No two climbers will experience the mountain in exactly the same way. Just as all of our beginnings are different, our ending will be different as well. What might be a minor obstacle for one could be a significant hurdle for another, depending on their physical conditioning, experience, and the equipment they carry. Similarly, in life, what constitutes a challenge for one person might be an easy task for another, influenced by their skills, support systems, and resources.

Along with the challenges of unpredictability, the act of comparing our journey to another's is a common trap that can significantly detract from personal fulfillment and happiness. We know the popular saying, "Comparison is the thief of joy," and this can be true especially in our ascent to the summit. This tendency to measure our progress against others overlooks the uniqueness of each individual's path—marked by distinct challenges, abilities, and circumstances. Just as in mountain climbing, where no two climbers can replicate each other's steps exactly due to differences in physicality, experience, and strategy, in life each person navigates their path based on a complex interplay of factors unique to them. Attempting to mimic another's journey or measuring our achievements against theirs is not only futile but can also diminish our sense of joy and accomplishment. Recognizing and embracing our unique journey, with all its intricacies, is essential for developing a healthier mindset and a richer perspective on life. It's crucial to understand that life is not a race or competition but a personal expedition where the true value lies in our individual experiences, growth, and the lessons we gather along the way. Embracing this perspective helps us appreciate our progress and celebrate our victories, no matter how different they may seem from those of others, ultimately leading to a more fulfilling and contented life.

The Summit: Achievements and New Perspectives

Reaching the summit of a mountain is often seen as the ultimate achievement, a tangible climax in the relentless journey of ascent. However, it is not just an end goal but a significant milestone that signals new insights, perspectives, and reflections. It's a point in the journey that allows climbers to pause, look back on the path they traversed, and appreciate the many challenges they have overcome and the lessons learned in the process. Similarly, in life, the peaks we reach—be they in our careers, personal development, relationships, or physical accomplishments—are not final destinations but pivotal moments that offer clarity, enlightenment, and a sense of achievement.

Reaching the summit can significantly shifts our perspective, both literally and metaphorically. From this elevated viewpoint, the world stretches out below, creating an extensive view that transforms our understanding of the journey. Literally instead of metaphorically, we often experience this viewpoint in planes, at sporting events, and in tall buildings when we feel as if everybody on the ground are ants. This physical change in perspective resembles a psychological shift, where the achievement of reaching the peak enlightens us on the importance of perspective in navigating life's challenges and appreciating its beauty.

This summit perspective allows us to see beyond the immediate challenges that once seemed unattainable, lighting the path we've taken with a clarity that can only be gained from such heights. It's a powerful reminder that the obstacles we face along the way are just parts of a larger landscape, each contributing to the journey's overall richness and depth. This broader view helps us appreciate the journey's intrinsic value, teaching us that every step, no matter how difficult, is essential to reaching our goals.

This enhanced perspective is not just about acknowledging our achievements but also about realizing the power of our viewpoint in shaping our experiences. It highlights the significance of adopting a mindset that values growth, resilience, and the journey itself over the appeal of reaching the peak. It teaches us that our perception of the climb, influenced by our attitudes and beliefs, can transform challenges into opportunities for learning and growth. It encourages a mindset shift from viewing achievements as final goals to seeing them as building blocks or vantage points from which to view the broader landscape of our lives. It motivates us to set new goals, seek new adventures, and continue the journey with renewed energy and a deeper understanding of what we are capable of achieving.

Now that the climber has reached the summit and look at the picturesque, view they realize they are surrounded by many other peaks that are a part of the same mountain range; some of which are higher than where they currently stand. Those other mountain peaks represent areas in our lives we were not aware of, other industries that we haven't become successful in yet, skills that we would like to master, relationships that are waiting to be strengthened, and unexplored opportunities. The summit that us as the climbers reached is just one of many that we choose from.

The realization that success in one area unveils new challenges and peaks in life is a testament to the dynamic and interconnected nature of our aspirations. The view from the summit thus becomes a metaphorical crossroads, where one achievement intersects with the potential for many more. It serves as the idea that every peak conquered is not an end but a vantage point for surveying the vast potential of what could be. This perspective highlights that life's journey is filled with multiple summits to strive for, each representing different aspects of our lives, whether it be in uncharted territories of our careers, deeper connections in our relationships, or untapped areas of personal development.

A perspective we can gain from reaching the summit is to acknowledge the importance of openness to new experiences and the willingness to venture into unknown realms. Just as the climber at the peak realizes the existence of higher mountains and unexplored paths, we too are encouraged to recognize the many opportunities that lie in pursuing areas of our lives that we have yet to explore. This expanded viewpoint creates a sense of curiosity and ambition, urging us to set our goals on new horizons with the same eagerness and discipline that brought us to our current peak.

This view from the top further enriches our understanding of how our perceptions shape our realities. It teaches us that our achievements are more than just endpoints, but stages for deeper exploration and self-discovery. This realization encourages a shift in perspective—from viewing success as a singular and finite goal to seeing it as a continuous, multifaceted journey. It is a reminder that with each summit reached, the landscape of our lives expands, revealing new paths to walk and new summits to reach.

The Descent: Maintenance, Challenges, and Balance

Everything that goes up must come down. Descending a mountain is a challenging phase of the journey, and it serves as a powerful metaphor for the intricacies of maintaining achievements in life. This phase of the climb requires as much, if not more, attention and skill as the ascent, emphasizing the need for precision and balance both physically and metaphorically. In the act of descending, climbers face increased physical demands, such as greater stress on the knees and the requirement for careful path selection to avoid slipping and falling. This physical challenge is similar to the often-underappreciated challenge of sustaining success in any aspect of life.

The summit is not to be perceived as being in the "prime" of your career or a period in time that you can't return to. It is more of a combination of achievements that previously were never crossed, to form a mountain range of the many moments in life. There are many examples of reaching this so-called summit. It can be in a career by achieving a dream job such as becoming CEO of a company, achieving tenure as a professor, or winning a prestigious award in a specific field. Also in personal health, with examples including recovering from a serious illness, completing a marathon, or achieving a personal fitness goal, like lifting, or losing a certain amount of weight. It can also be in relationships, such as celebrating an anniversary, successfully navigating a tough period with a partner or family member, or just strengthening and creating an even more supportive environment.

Once a peak is reached, the effort shifts from reaching to maintaining that success. This shift is not hardly a passive state but an active and dynamic process, with potential pitfalls and the need for constant mind-fulness and adjustment. Just as descending a mountain requires a climber to be keenly aware of each step, maintaining success in life demands continuous efforts and strategic planning. The descent highlights the elevated consequences of mistakes; a misstep on the way down can have more severe repercussions than a similar mistake on the way up. This mirrors the reality that losing ground, once a certain level of achievement has been reached, can feel more significant and have more substantial consequences than the challenges faced on the way to success.

In addition, descending effectively requires a shift in perspective. Climbers must look at the path ahead from a different angle, focusing more directly and immediately on the terrain beneath their feet rather than the distant summit. This change in focus is critical for safely navigating the way down, requiring a balance of confidence and caution. In life, this translates to a perspective where past achievements are not merely milestones but also platforms for future action. It involves recognizing that past success does not guarantee future progress without continued effort, adaptation, and discipline.

The necessity for precision and balance in the descent also highlights the importance of humility and readiness to adjust. Just as climbers must adapt their pace and technique to safely reach the bottom, we must continually adapt our strategies to maintain our achievements and respond to new challenges. This perspective encourages a proactive approach to life's descent phases, emphasizing that success is not static but an ongoing journey of adaptation and careful management.

In this chapter, we explored life's journey through the metaphor of climbing a mountain, focusing on the multitude of small steps, strategic breaks, and continuous adjustments that define our path to the summit. By not fixating on the peak but rather concentrating on the journey itself, we can see the importance of each decision—where to pause, whom we journey with, and how we adapt to challenges like unpredictable weather or physical limitations. This highlights the significance of preparation, adaptability, and the mindful use of resources, paralleling these climbing strategies with life's broader challenges. As we reach each summit, we gain not only a moment of achievement but also a broadened perspective that reveals new peaks and possibilities, encouraging a shift in focus from achieving to maintaining. The descent is often more challenging than the ascent, and it requires precision, balance, and strategic foresight, emphasizing the ongoing effort needed to sustain our gains and navigate future paths. This journey through climbing teaches us the value of perspective in appreciating our individual paths and the interconnected nature of our goals, driving home the idea that life, much like climbing, is not a singular climb to the top but a continuous series of ascents and descents, each with valuable lessons and opportunities.

> "It is not the mountain we conquer, but ourselves."
> —Sir Edmund Hillary

3
The War Room
The Battle Within

Welcome to the War Room. This isn't a place; it's a state of mind. Every victory you seek and every challenge you will face starts here. This is where the real fight begins—before you take a single step toward your goals, before you make a single move in the world. It all starts in your mind. Your mind is the battlefield, and every decision, every thought, is a fight for control. *Master the war within, and the rest of your life will fall into place.* This is where strength is forged, where limits are shattered, and where success is born.

But the battles we fight within ourselves can often feel like the hardest to win. For many of us, the loudest and most persistent adversary is our own inner critic. It whispers—or shouts—labels like "awkward," "boring," or "not enough," reinforcing a sense of inadequacy that keeps us stuck in a mental spiral. These labels often stem from deep-rooted shame and criticism, echoing back to childhood. These self-critical narratives often form in environments where shame or a lack of validation was common. Over time these labels transform into belief systems that dictate how we see ourselves, limiting not only our self-worth but also our choices and relationships.

The battle within often arises when our desires, fears, and doubts clash with the guidance of our inner compass. It's the internal tug-of-war between what we *think* we should do and what our deeper wisdom knows is right for us. This internal conflict can create confusion and tension, pulling us in different directions and leaving us uncertain about which path to take. Yet, the battle within doesn't have to be a struggle—it can be an invitation to reconnect with our inner compass.

Psychologist Ellen Hendriksen describes this phenomenon as a fear of exposure—a belief that our flaws are so glaring that if revealed, they will lead to rejection or judgment. This fear can be paralyzing, convincing us to avoid risks, relationships, and opportunities in favor of staying "safe" in familiar, albeit unfulfilling, patterns. Yet this safety comes at a steep cost. The more we avoid stepping into uncertainty, the more we reinforce the narrative of our inner critic.[1] It becomes a vicious cycle, where every mistake is seen as proof of inadequacy, and every success is dismissed as mere luck.

Interestingly, not all self-doubt is harmful. In its healthy form, self-doubt serves as a tool for self-regulation, allowing us to monitor our behavior and build stronger relationships. Hendriksen describes it as "doubting ourselves to check ourselves," a mechanism that keeps us attuned to others and grounded in social interactions. However, when self-doubt takes the form of perfectionism, it shifts from being a helpful guide to a relentless critic. Perfectionism, as Hendriksen explains, isn't about striving for excellence but rather about feeling perpetually "less-than." It amplifies anxiety, undermines confidence, and traps us in an exhausting loop of never feeling good enough.

The way out of this mental battleground begins with reclaiming control over the narrative. By practicing self-compassion, we can begin to view ourselves with greater objectivity, dismantling shame-based labels and replacing them with a more balanced and accepting self-perception. At the same time, Hendriksen advocates for stepping into action, even when fear and doubt persist. She argues that confidence doesn't come first; it grows through action. Taking small, deliberate steps toward the things we fear helps reframe the story we tell ourselves, proving that we are more capable than our inner critic would have us believe.

The battles within our minds are inevitable, but they are also winnable. Recognizing the inner critic for what it is—a misguided attempt to protect us—is the first step. From there, arming ourselves with self-compassion and embracing the discomfort of imperfection allows us to move forward despite fear. The War Room is not just where battles are fought; it's where victories are planned and won. This is where strength is forged, where limits are shattered, and where success is born. The tools to reclaim your mind are within reach. The question is: Are you ready to pick them up?

In life, you're either the thermostat or the thermometer. You're either setting the temperature or reacting to it. Which one are you? Are you shaping your destiny, or just letting life happen to you? Being mediocre isn't an option. Being a loser isn't an option. Not having enough isn't an option. It's time to rise. Being at the bottom isn't acceptable anymore. Get up. *Obsession is what separates the average from the excellent.* Be obsessed, or be average. Being average isn't going to cut it anymore. Tell yourself that you're done letting things slide. Obsession is your key to breaking through. Keep pushing.

If you're just reacting to what life throws at you, you've already lost. People who sit around waiting for things to change don't get anywhere. They stay stuck. If you want something, you better decide that you're the one calling the shots. You better set the temperature in your life, or someone else will do it for you. Waiting around, hoping things will get better, is for losers. Get up and make things happen!

Ever said these defeating words? "I can't yet." "I don't want to." "I don't feel like it today." "I'll do it later." Stop being weak, and toughen up. If you really wanted it, you'd already be chasing it. Stop making excuses. If you want something, go and get it. Excuses are pathetic. If being weak is your plan, then sit down and stay out of the way.

Look, everyone's got reasons why they can't do things. But guess what? No one truly cares. Your excuses are irrelevant to the world. If you really want something, no excuse will ever be big enough to stop you. If you're tired? Too bad. Get up and do it anyway. If you don't feel like it? Too bad. You don't get to wait for the perfect conditions, because they don't exist. No one is handing out success because you had a tough day. The difference between winners and losers is that winners show up anyway. They grind when others quit. They push when their body says no, when their mind says it's too hard. Losers sit back and justify their failure with excuses. Which one are you?

Stop Lying to Yourself

The hard truth is that life owes you nothing. It's a battleground, and if you don't show up ready to fight, you're going to lose. Every single day you wake up to a choice: stay where you are, or push forward. The world doesn't care about your excuses, your setbacks, or your reasons why things didn't work out. It only rewards action. If you want something, you have to earn it. Most successful people weren't handed that life. They didn't wake up with a million followers, a perfect body, or a thriving business. They worked for it. While you were sleeping in, they were grinding. While you were making excuses, they were making progress.

Stop lying to yourself. You know the truth. You know whether you are giving it everything you've got or just coasting. If you're not where you want to be, it's not because of bad luck or other people holding you back—it's because you're not doing enough. The problem isn't out there. The problem is you. You've got to look in the mirror and ask yourself, "Am I really doing everything I can? Am I leaving anything on the table?" If the answer is yes, then step up. You got this. Listening to the compass within strengthens your ability to lead your life with intention. If you don't have a plan and let life happen to you instead, then you will never activate your purpose and passion.

"I am not what happened to me, I am what I choose to become." —Carl Yung

Tiger Woods said it best: "Nothing's ever going to be given to you. Everything's going to be earned. If you don't go out there and put in the work . . . you don't deserve it. You need to earn it."[2] You think you deserve success just because you want it? No. The universe doesn't care about your desires—it responds to your actions. You either put in the work, or you don't. You either earn it, or you don't.

You can't dip your toes in the water and expect to swim with the sharks. You have to dive in. Half-assing your way through life will get you nowhere. You think people at the top are just going through the motions? No. They're obsessed. They eat, sleep, and breathe their goals. It's not just something they do when it's convenient; it's their life. You want to be the best? You better make it your obsession. The truth is, mediocrity is comfortable. It's easy to coast along, doing just enough to get by. But that's not going to cut it. You either become obsessed with your goals, or you stay stuck where you are—average and forgotten. You want to leave a mark? You want to be remembered? Then be obsessed. There is no other option.

Prepare for the Daily Battles and the Occasional Storms

Make it or break it. You win or lose based on the daily battles. The big goals, the massive dreams don't get achieved in a single moment. They're the result of showing up every day and doing the work, no matter how you feel, no matter what else is going on. Win those daily battles, and the war will take care of itself. You think success is some big, magical moment? It's not. It's the result of all the small, unglamorous, gritty things you do every day. The real winners aren't the ones who just show up when it's easy or when they feel like it. They are the ones who win the daily battles when no one's watching. The ones who push when they're tired, when they're sore, when everything in them is screaming to quit. That's where success is made. Every single day is a battle. You're either going to win it or lose it. You're either going to show up and give it everything you've got, or you're going to let the day beat you down. Success is about accumulating those wins. Day after day, you win the small battles, and before you know it, you've won the war. But if you keep losing those daily battles, don't be surprised when you're still stuck in the same place years from now.

Stop running from the hard stuff. Be like the buffalo in the storm: run straight into it. When you face challenges head-on, you come out stronger on the other side. Running away is for the weak. Running toward the storm? That's where the growth happens. That's where you separate yourself from the pack. The easy road leads nowhere. It's the hard path, the one filled with obstacles and setbacks, that leads to real success. Growth doesn't happen when things are easy. You don't grow in comfort. You grow in the storm, in the discomfort, in the pain. That's where you find out who you really are. That's where champions are made. If you keep running from every challenge, every tough situation, you're robbing yourself of the chance to become stronger. You're staying weak.

You need to embrace the struggle, not avoid it. Every time you feel like quitting, every time things get hard, that's where the growth happens. You can't cheat the process. The more storms you face, the stronger you get. The more you run into the fire, the more fireproof you become. So stop running. Face it head-on and conquer it.

Imbalance Prepares Us for the Unexpected

Elon Musk doesn't just talk about hard work—he embodies it. With a relentless schedule of eighty to one hundred hours a week, he proves that success isn't about waiting for opportunities; it's about creating them. Musk isn't sitting back, hoping for things to happen. He's out there pushing harder than anyone else because he knows one undeniable truth: Effort is everything. While others clock out at forty hours, Musk keeps grinding, understanding that the more you put in, the more you get out. He's not chasing success; he's outworking everyone to make it happen.

Balance is not the key. If you want to be the best, you can't have balance. There will be times when you're fully obsessed, when you give everything to your craft, and other things in your life will take a back seat. That's okay. Greatness demands imbalance. It demands sacrifice. You can balance things out once you've won. Until then, it's all or nothing. Balance is a myth. You think people who reach the top are balancing everything perfectly? No. They're putting everything they've got into their craft.

They're letting other things slide because they're obsessed with being the best. Balance is for people who are fine with mediocrity. You want to be the best? You've got to be unbalanced for a while. There's time to relax later. Right now, you grind.

Embrace the Struggle

Jocko Willink summarized this well: "Didn't get what you wanted? Good. That means there's more work to be done. Got knocked down? Good. That's an opportunity to get back up stronger. Life isn't supposed to be easy. The struggle is the point. Every time something goes wrong, that's a chance to get better, to learn, to grow. You need the setbacks. You need the failures. They're part of your path to success.

Every time life throws things at you, say, "Good." Didn't get the promotion? *Good.* Time to work harder. Got rejected? *Good.* Time to get better. Life isn't meant to be smooth sailing. The struggle is where the real growth happens. Every setback is a lesson; every failure is an opportunity to level up. Winners don't cry about what went wrong. They use it to get stronger. You're not a victim; you're a warrior. And the struggle is just part of your journey.

The internal war is the only one that matters. Everything else is secondary. You can blame the world, blame your circumstances, blame other people, but at the end of the day, it's you versus you. You either win the battle against your own mind, or you lose. And if you lose that battle, nothing else matters. The real war is in your head. *You are your biggest enemy and your greatest ally.* It's not the world, it's not other people, it's not circumstances—it's you. The voice in your head telling you to quit, to take it easy, to stop—that's the real enemy. But the voice telling you to push harder, to keep going when it gets tough—that's your greatest ally. You've got to shut down the doubt and amplify the strength. You've got to be stronger than the excuses your mind feeds you. You've got to fight every day to win that internal war, because once you do, the rest of the world doesn't stand a chance.

Wake up every day with the intent to win. The moment you open your eyes, you're in the fight. It's not about motivation—it's about discipline. Motivation fades. Discipline stays. Discipline is what gets you out of bed when you're exhausted, what keeps you grinding when you're not seeing results, what pushes you forward when everyone else is slowing down. Motivation is temporary. It's easy to feel motivated when things are going well. But what happens when it gets tough? What happens when the excitement wears off? That's when discipline kicks in. Discipline is what makes you show up when motivation has disappeared. Discipline is what gets you through the hard days, the long nights, the setbacks, and the failures.

This is the War Room. The battle is fought and won in your mind long before you ever see the results in your life. Get your mind right, and the rest will follow.

> *"You have the power over your mind—not outside events. Realize this, and you will find strength." —Marcus Aurelius*

4
Motivation vs. Discipline
Why Consistency Outlasts Excitement

Motivation is exciting. It's the spark that gets you out of bed, fills you with energy, and pushes you to start chasing your goals. But here's the harsh truth: Motivation is fleeting. It fades when the excitement wears off or when life throws obstacles in your path. Discipline, on the other hand, is the engine that keeps you moving forward—long after motivation has disappeared.

Discipline, when guided by our compass within, becomes a tool for focused action that is in harmony with our values and goals. Instead of feeling like a rigid set of rules or external control, discipline rooted in the inner compass is an act of self-trust. It's the commitment to follow through on what truly matters, guided by the clarity of our inner wisdom. When we align discipline with our inner compass, we cultivate the ability to stay on track, not out of obligation or fear, but because our actions resonate deeply with our true purpose.

Jocko Willink, the legendary Navy SEAL and leadership expert, captures this perfectly. He's often asked, "How do I build discipline in my life?" His answer is as straightforward as it is unappealing to those looking for shortcuts: *Start with the basics, like waking up early. That's where it all begins. When the alarm goes off, resist the temptation to hit the snooze button.* For Willink, every time you choose discipline over comfort, you reinforce your commitment to your goals. It's not about grand gestures but small, consistent actions that build momentum. The snooze button is the ultimate "dream killer."[1] Each time you hit it, you're putting off your dreams just a little longer. Discipline is what gets you out of bed on the days when you'd rather stay under the covers. It's what pushes you to keep going when the excitement has faded, exhaustion has set in, and the challenges feel overwhelming. Motivation might get you to the starting line, but discipline is what carries you to the finish.

David Goggins, a man who embodies relentless discipline, goes even further. He doesn't mince words when he says, "Motivation is crap."[2] Goggins believes that relying on motivation is a recipe for failure because it's dependent on how you feel in the moment—and feelings are unreliable. True progress, he argues, comes from obsession and commitment. It's about showing up and doing the work, even when every fiber of your being is screaming for you to stop. That's the difference between those who talk about success and those who achieve it: the willingness to push through discomfort and execute consistently.

This is where discipline reveals its transformative power. It's not just about willpower; it's about creating systems and routines that make action inevitable. When you practice discipline daily, your brain begins to normalize these behaviors. Actions that once felt challenging become second nature. Willink emphasizes that discipline creates freedom—freedom from the chaos of procrastination, indecision, and the constant search for motivation. By sticking to disciplined actions, you train your brain to see possibilities where before you only saw obstacles.

Steven Bartlett, an entrepreneur and author, takes this idea further, framing discipline as a formula: the strength of your why plus the reward of the behavior minus the cost of inaction.[3] When you're clear on why you're doing something and what it will bring you, discipline becomes easier to sustain. Bartlett reminds us that discipline isn't about waiting for the perfect moment or a surge of motivation; it's about taking action because you've decided it's nonnegotiable.

Think of discipline as a muscle. The more you use it, the stronger it gets. Every time you resist the urge to procrastinate or choose discomfort over ease, you're reinforcing your commitment to your goals. The beauty of discipline is that it grows through repetition. The more you practice it, the less you need to rely on fleeting motivation. Eventually, discipline becomes automatic—a habit embedded in your daily life, driving you forward no matter what.

This mindset shift is crucial. Instead of seeing discipline as restrictive or burdensome, view it as a tool that empowers you to achieve your dreams. It's not about punishing yourself; it's about building the life you want, one decision at a time. Success isn't achieved through bursts of excitement or occasional effort. It's earned through the grind, through showing up day after day, and through choosing discipline over comfort.

Discipline is the bridge between who you are and who you want to become. Cross it daily.

In the end, discipline isn't just about action; it's about identity. It's the difference between saying, "I want to be successful," and *being* the kind of person who shows up, puts in the work, and refuses to quit. Discipline is the engine that drives results, and it's the most reliable tool you have on the journey to greatness.

The Illusion of Motivation vs. the Power of Action

Motivation often feels like progress. It's exciting to write down goals, make to-do lists, and talk about ambitions. But this kind of preparation, while important, can create the illusion of progress without real action. Chris Williamson, a thought leader on performance and growth, points out a critical truth: "Preparing to do the thing isn't doing the thing. Scheduling time to do the thing isn't doing the thing. Making a to-do list for the thing isn't doing the thing. Telling people you are going to do the thing isn't doing the thing."[4] Motivation might inspire you to create a plan, but only discipline ensures you execute it.

The problem with relying on motivation is that it's tied to emotion, and emotions are fleeting. The people who achieve their goals are those who move beyond the planning and dreaming phase into relentless execution. They don't wait to feel ready—they act because they understand that real progress only happens through consistent effort.

Taking action creates a feedback loop. The more you do, the more momentum you build, the easier it becomes to keep going. By consistently showing up and putting in the work, you start to see real progress. Your brain begins to associate action with results, and over time the resistance to starting diminishes. What was once hard becomes routine, and what was once daunting becomes achievable.

The illusion of motivation is seductive because it feels good in the moment. But the people who truly succeed understand that feeling good isn't the goal—getting results is. Discipline ensures that you move beyond the planning phase into consistent, meaningful action. It's the antidote to procrastination and the key to unlocking your potential.

By focusing on action rather than waiting for motivation, you start to shift your mindset. You stop seeing obstacles as insurmountable and start viewing them as challenges to overcome. This shift is what leads to long-term success. Discipline doesn't just get you started; it carries you through the hard days and ensures you stay in the game long enough to see results.

The Role of Routines: Stability and Momentum

Discipline thrives on consistency, and nothing creates consistency like a well-structured routine. Routines are more than just schedules. They are frameworks that guide your actions, remove emotional decision-making, and keep you moving toward your goals, regardless of how you feel. When discipline feels like an uphill battle, routines provide the stability to carry you forward.

A well-designed life is the result of disciplined, consistent actions. Routines serve as the building blocks of this process, creating a structure that ensures progress. By establishing daily habits that align with your goals, you transform discipline into a way of life, not just an occasional effort. Bedros Keuilian, a successful entrepreneur and performance coach, illustrates the power of routines with his strict morning ritual. Every day, he wakes up early, drinks thirty ounces of water, sends gratitude messages, and starts his "GSD" (Get Shit Done) list.[5] This routine isn't about perfection; it's about removing decision fatigue. By following the same steps every morning, Keuilian eliminates the temptation to negotiate with himself and ensures his day begins with productivity and focus.

Routines create predictability, which is a powerful antidote to the chaos of distractions and challenges. They act as anchors, helping you maintain momentum even when life feels overwhelming. When you build a routine that aligns with your goals, you ensure that your actions are deliberate and purposeful, not reactive. Michael Phelps, the most decorated Olympian in history, offers another powerful example of the importance of routines. For five years, Phelps trained every single day without missing a workout. His rationale was simple: in swimming, missing one day sets you back two. By showing up daily, regardless of how he felt, Phelps built an unbreakable foundation of consistency. His routine eliminated the guesswork and ensured that his discipline remained intact, even on the hardest days.

"I trained four years to run nine seconds." —Usain Bolt

The beauty of routines lies in their compounding effect. Each day's actions build on the previous day's efforts, creating a sense of progress and accomplishment. Over time, these small, consistent actions lead to massive results. Transformation isn't about grand gestures; it's about micro-actions repeated over time. Even when progress feels slow or invisible, routines ensure you stay on track, trusting the process.

Routines also help you manage emotional fluctuations and remove the need for constant negotiation with yourself. You don't have to decide whether to work out, tackle your to-do list, or make time for your goals. Those decisions have already been made by your routine. This predictability allows you to focus on execution, not excuses. But routines are not just about productivity; they're about stability. They give your life a sense of control, even in the face of uncertainty. When you know what to expect from your day, you're better equipped to handle the unexpected. Routines create a foundation that allows you to adapt without losing momentum.

Discipline becomes second nature when it's tied to a routine. The more you stick to your habits, the more ingrained they become, turning once-difficult tasks into automatic behaviors. This is the secret to maintaining momentum: by relying on routines, you eliminate the emotional highs and lows that can derail progress. Instead, you create a steady rhythm that carries you toward your goals, one day at a time.

Incorporating a routine into your life isn't about rigidity; it's about empowerment. It's about taking control of your actions and ensuring that every day contributes to your success. As Jim Rohn said, "Discipline is the bridge between goals and accomplishment."[6] And that bridge is built, step by step, through the power of routine. Routines also create the compounding effect of small wins. Success doesn't come from big, grand actions; it's the result of small, consistent habits you build every day. Consider this:

- Saving $8 a day adds up to almost $3,000 a year.
- Reading twenty pages a day means you'll finish 30 books in a year.
- Walking 10,000 steps a day is equivalent to completing seventy marathons a year.

Nonnegotiable Commitments: Building Self-Trust

The most successful people don't negotiate with themselves. Once a goal is set, it becomes a contract—not something to be debated based on how they feel that day. Discipline is about honoring these commitments to yourself, even when it's uncomfortable. By making your actions nonnegotiable, you develop a mindset that views success as inevitable, not optional.

Kobe Bryant, a legendary example of this principle, once said, "The deal was already made when I set [the goal]."[7] For him, there was no room for second-guessing or renegotiating, no matter how hard it got. When he planned his summer training, that plan became set in stone. Bryant understood that success demands consistency, not convenience. He treated his commitments as sacred, knowing that every skipped workout or half-hearted effort would chip away at the foundation of his goals.

This unwavering mindset transforms how you view discipline. It's no longer about doing things when it's easy or when you feel like it; it's about showing up because you promised yourself you would. When you honor your commitments, you reinforce your self-trust. Each follow-through becomes a building block of confidence and resilience.

Connor McGregor, the champion MMA fighter, embodies this same principle. He stresses the importance of keeping promises to yourself, no matter how small. If you commit to training at a specific time, you train. If you decide to eat clean, you follow through. McGregor warns that every time you fail to honor your word to yourself, you're stacking defeats instead of victories. Each broken promise erodes your mental strength and self-belief, while every fulfilled commitment builds a foundation of success.

Discipline removes emotion from the equation. It's not about how you feel; it's about what you've decided. Your feelings in the moment are fleeting, but the decisions you make and stick to shape your future. By committing to the work regardless of mood or external circumstances, you shift your perspective. Tasks are no longer optional or burdensome; they become the essential steps toward the life you want. This approach creates a domino effect. When you start treating your commitments as nonnegotiable, you begin to see tasks as opportunities rather than obligations. Each completed task reinforces your belief in yourself, creating a cycle of progress and achievement. Over time, this self-trust becomes a powerful driver of discipline. You're no longer fighting to stay motivated because your identity shifts. You become the kind of person who keeps promises to themselves.

Building this level of discipline doesn't require perfection; it requires consistency. Transformation happens through small, consistent actions. Whether it's showing up to the gym, sticking to a morning routine, or following through on a work commitment, each action strengthens your ability to perform without excuses. Michael Phelps's legendary consistency highlights this point. He trained every day for five years, never missing a session. Phelps didn't negotiate with himself about whether he felt like swimming. He just swam. This relentless discipline wasn't about short-term goals; it was about building a foundation of trust in himself and his process. The result? Unmatched success and an enduring legacy.

Nonnegotiable commitments also protect you from the distractions and temptations that derail so many people. When a goal is set and the path to achieving it is clear, there's no room for excuses or shortcuts. You begin to see your goals as promises you've made to yourself, and breaking them is no longer an option.

Ultimately, discipline isn't about willpower; it's about identity. It's about becoming the kind of person who does what they say they will do. As Kobe Bryant put it, "The deal was already made."[8] By making your commitments nonnegotiable, you align your actions with your ambitions, creating a life of consistency, growth, and success. Over time, these small, consistent victories add up, transforming your mindset and solidifying your path to greatness.

5
The Winning Effect
Momentum in Motion

When a person wins a contest, there is a large release of dopamine and testosterone in their brain. Over time this changes the chemical makeup and structure of the brain, making the person smarter, more confident, and more willing to take on larger challenges then they did previously. There are many reasons why we should acknowledge and reward our small and daily wins, some of which include: boosting motivation, building self-confidence, developing a growth mindset, maintaining momentum, improving well-being, increasing productivity, and building a positive culture.

The winning effect is one of my favorite concepts because of its incredible practicality. Every day, I intentionally plan and seek out small wins that I can achieve, knowing that each one compounds into something greater. It's a mindset that starts the night before, just like how my grandmama used to prepare her meals—letting flavors marinate overnight for maximum impact. I take the same approach with my discipline, setting myself up for success in ways that might seem small but build unstoppable momentum. For example, I prepare for the next day by taking amino acids to help my body recover—a small win. I lay out my gym clothes and school outfits so I can start the morning without hesitation—a small win. Each morning, I drink a "green drink" with probiotics and big glasses of water—a small win. I never miss my 7:45 a.m. and 8:30 a.m. classes, no matter how tired I may feel—a small win.

These small, daily wins extend beyond routines. I hit the gym every day except Sunday. I've trained jiu-jitsu at least twice a week for two years straight (two to six hours a week). I dedicated time to work on this book for at least two hours a day. For an entire year, I wrote one verse of Scripture every single day on a sticky note and stuck them neatly in a row, creating a "Scripture wall." These practices might sound ordinary, but they create an extraordinary effect. Each win builds on the last, creating a snowball of momentum that drives me forward. Even when I hit a slump, I've created so many avenues to achieve small victories that it's easy to get back into a winning mindset. It's like compound interest for personal growth: one win fuels the next, and the cycle continues, reinforcing confidence, discipline, and progress. This is the essence of the winning effect—finding ways to succeed in the small, knowing they lead to the monumental.

> *"Success doesn't come from what you do occasionally, it comes from what you do consistently."* —Marie Forleo

There is a societal concept of accumulated advantage called the Matthew Effect. Those that start with an advantage will accrue more of that advantage. This concept stems from Matthew 25:29: "For whosoever hath, to him shall be given, and he shall have more abundance: but whosoever hath not, from him shall be taken away even that he hath." This means, to those who have more, more will be given, and from those who have nothing, everything will be taken. This implies that those who are in advantage when it comes to wealth, fame, intelligence, resources, and overall success, are more likely to gain more of that advantage, while those who lack such advantages may struggle in improving the card that they were dealt and may experience even further setbacks.

Momentum is the force that propels us forward, and when it aligns with our inner compass, it becomes a powerful tool for progress. Our inner compass serves as the source of clarity, helping us understand where we want to go and why it matters. Once we tune in to its guidance, we can build momentum that is both purposeful and sustainable—driven not by external pressures or fleeting motivation, but by our deepest values and desires. When we trust our inner compass, momentum no longer feels like a struggle to keep going. Instead, it becomes a natural flow—a rhythm of action that feels aligned with who we are and where we want to go. Every step we take becomes part of a larger, meaningful journey, and our inner compass keeps us on course, even when external distractions or challenges arise.

Many of us know of the common phrase, "The rich get richer, and the poor get poorer." Economists use this principle to describe how the economy in the world works. Wealth inequality is one way we see this principle. Individuals or groups with access to capital, education, networks, and other resources often have a greater ability to generate income and accumulate wealth. As they accumulate more wealth, they gain access to additional opportunities for investment, increased income, and asset accumulation, creating a cycle of increasing success. Conversely, individuals or groups facing economic disadvantages, such as limited access to education, job opportunities, or financial resources, may find it challenging to escape poverty or improve their economic status. Some barriers of breaking this cycle may include difficulty in accessing credit, investing in education or training, or starting a business, which perpetuates this cycle of disadvantage.

There is an interesting philosophy that I adopted and started to integrate into my life from Tim Grover, motivational speaker and owner of Attack Athletics. He believes we all know there is a price we must pay for winning, but most people are not willing to pay that price. People also may pay it one time, but this is not that type of choice. You have to pay this price every single day. The crazy part is that the price changes every day, just how the stock market goes up and down.[1] We must understand that the price of winning changes on a daily basis and we have to be willing to pay that price regardless of the day. The reason why the price changes is because the reward does as well. We see this in our daily lives. One day we might have a presentation due for a job or class, and the reward for this is different than a reward for being promoted to a blue belt in jiu jitsu. Our daily schedules may contain similarity, but we all incorporate some sort of variation as we are all unique.

One day I might have a very important basketball game because I know college coaches are in attendance. One day I might have a judo belt promotion, which means I must be prepared to identify throwing techniques or positional holds in Japanese, translate them into English, and then be able to execute. One day I might have an interview with Stanford or Dartmouth during the college admissions process. One day I might . . . and on it goes. Whatever each of our situations are, there is a price to be paid in accordance with the outcomes of our desired goals. Some will shoot farther and higher than others, some will just try to be better than they were yesterday, and some will try to maintain where they are currently.

The winning effect incorporates psychological and emotional benefits such as increased confidence and motivation, while also enhancing behavioral and cognitive functions like improved focus and self-trust, influencing social dynamics and interpersonal relationships positively; however, it also presents challenges such as the risk of pressure and burnout. Ultimately, understanding and harnessing the winning effect allows us to refine perspectives that prioritize growth, balance, and holistic well-being, paving the way for sustainable success and achievement in various aspects of life.

Boost Confidence and Self-Esteem Through Winning

Within the winning effect, there are several easy ways that it plays a role in our perspectives. One of which is through psychological and emotion impacts in the examples of confidence, motivation, and the reduction of stress. Most of us have experienced some sort of win. Whether it's winning a simple game of Kahoot or scoring a touchdown, we are designed to associate positive emotions with winning through the release of dopamine. Dopamine is a neurotransmitter, or chemical messenger, that is made in your brain and is known as the reward center. It has multiple functions including memory, motivation, and mood.

In the context of confidence, dopamine can be referred to as the "feel good" neurotransmitter because it is associated with pleasure, reward, and reinforcement. When dopamine levels are elevated, such as when we win in competition or experience our perception of success, it can contribute to increased feelings of confidence and self-assurance. Dopamine reinforces positive behaviors and experiences, which leads to a higher and higher probability of future success. In the context of motivation, dopamine is closely related. When dopamine levels rise in response to an anticipated reward or success, it enhances our motivation to continue to carry out behaviors that will likely lead to a similar positive outcome in the future. In this, we are constantly engaging with our perceptions of what success is and our reaction to achieving it. To the degree in which we enjoy and value that definition of success, our levels of motivation toward it will vary in accordance.

Dopamine can help mitigate the effects of stress and anxiety. When we are able to maintain balanced levels of dopamine, it can counteract the negative effects of stress by promoting feelings of calm and resilience. The sense of winning or accomplishment that is associated with dopamine release can serve as a cushion against stressors, helping us to handle challenging situations more effectively. Through this we are able to engage with each of our definitions of stress and anxiety, knowing how we were able to handle and overcome challenges that were similar in the past.

- Success breeds confidence.
- Success breeds success.
- Reps remove doubt.

Behavioral and Cognitive Effects of Winning

Another way that the winning effect plays a role in our perception is through various behavioral and cognitive effects. Some include increased focus, rewarding ourselves, and building self-trust. Stacking your wins aligns with all three elements of the behavioral and cognitive influence that the winning effect has. People always wonder if there is one thing that they should focus on that will grant them success. This is as if they believe there is only this one big win. He goes through examples of little wins that we can achieve throughout the day to keep our behaviors in check and build winning habits.[3]

One example is asking, "Did you hit the snooze button this morning?" If the answer is no, then you stacked a loss instead of a win. One thing we all can do in the morning is not hit the snooze button. And then get up when the alarm goes off, or even get up before it goes off. In doing so, we are able to get a win, and we should be proud of ourselves that we can start the day off already ahead. Another win could be to drink water to rehydrate ourselves right after waking. If we are able to do this, now we are at two back-to-back wins. If not, then we are back to zero wins. Another win could be not checking social media for an hour after we wake up. Instead, maybe we could take a shower, get a workout in, journal, read a book, meditate, or do yoga. We should have a plan to GSD (Get Shit Done). Now we should do the same thing the next hour, and the next hour, and the next hour. Stacking those little wins over time is so important. There is not a moment in time where we go from a white belt to a black belt in jiu jitsu overnight. Great things take time!

> "Small disciplines repeated with consistency every day lead to great achievements over time." —John C. Maxwell

Rewarding ourselves can also be a byproduct of the winning effect when it comes to behavioral and cognitive influences. To build on this idea there is a segment where Andrew Huberman, neuroscientist and podcaster, describes the process of self-reward. He suggests that the most powerful tool we have is the ability to internally reward ourselves. This means acknowledging our progress and successes along the way, rather than solely focusing on the final outcome. By recognizing our efforts and telling ourselves that we're on the right path, we can activate a positive feedback loop that fuels our energy and focus. Huberman emphasizes that this internal reward system is crucial for maintaining motivation and perseverance, as it helps to counteract the natural tendency to quit when faced with challenges.[2]

Our varying perspectives on life play a significant role in how we reward ourselves internally. Individuals with a growth mindset, for example, are more likely to view challenges as opportunities for learning and growth. They may reward themselves for their efforts and progress, even if they haven't yet achieved their ultimate goals. On the other hand, individuals with a fixed mindset may be more focused on external validation and success, leading them to withhold rewards until they achieve a specific outcome.

Cultural factors also influence how we reward ourselves internally. In cultures that prioritize individual achievement and success, individuals may place a greater emphasis on external validation and tangible rewards. In contrast, cultures that value community, collaboration, and personal development may place more emphasis on internal measures of success, such as personal growth and fulfillment.

Our past experiences and upbringing shape our beliefs about self-worth and success, which in turn influence how we reward ourselves internally. Individuals who have experienced consistent praise and encouragement may be more adept at self-reward and self-motivation, while those who have faced criticism or setbacks may struggle to recognize their own accomplishments.

Build Self-Trust and Identity Through Consistency

As previously mentioned, it is best to start with easy wins so they will stack and compound to create momentum. The same is true when it comes to building trust within self. Entrepreneur Luke Belmar created an interesting scene to illustrate this. He said, "If I told you every single day that we were gonna go to the gym, and I didn't show up, but you showed up. On the tenth day would you believe me? The answer would be not a chance. Would you trust me? The answer is no. This is the problem where most people don't trust themselves because they are in auto self-sabotage mode twenty-four seven. No wonder why you don't have any courage, no wonder

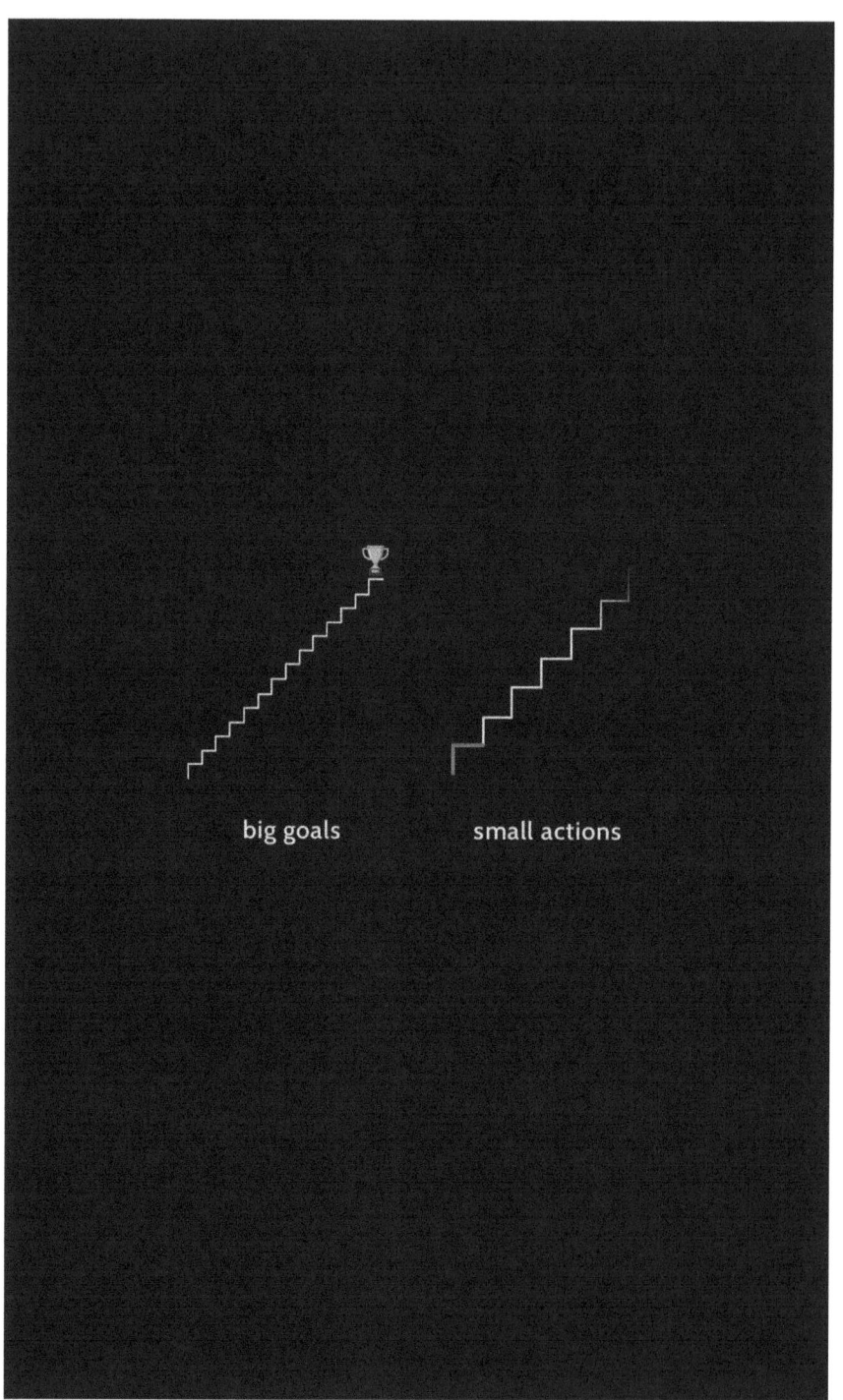

big goals   small actions

you think you're going to fail, your mind is really saying, *I can't trust you*, so you need to start on small wins."[3] Clean your room, get dressed, start hanging out with good people, read a chapter in a book. When you say, "I'm going to read a chapter," you sit down and you read it. Through this, you start building trust with yourself and then you realize, *Wow, I can actually do anything that I want.*

This is very true as building self-trust is essential for personal growth and success. Often our lack of self-trust stems from repeatedly breaking promises to ourselves, which erodes our confidence and belief in our abilities. To build self-trust, it's important to start with achievable goals or "easy wins" that we can consistently follow through on. This could involve simple tasks like making your bed every morning, spending a few minutes organizing an area of your home, preparing your clothes for the next day the night before, choosing a healthy meal, or committing to small daily habits like reading a chapter of a book or going to the gym. By setting and accomplishing these small goals, we demonstrate to ourselves that we are capable of keeping our word and following through on commitments. Each success builds momentum and reinforces our belief in our ability to achieve more significant objectives.

There is also a concept I build upon from entrepreneur and author Wes Watson: "I am a man of my word." He said that he's a man of his thoughts. If he thinks about it, he makes it happen.[4] In a positive narrative this can be very powerful. In my case, I have found myself doing this as well. For example, when it came to the idea of writing this book, I never told anybody that I would write it. Yet, alone, before I graduate college. I joked with my dad and some of my close friends, saying, "Wow, one day that would be such a huge accomplishment." After I do this, this, and this, I'll have an interesting story to talk about. During those moments my perspective changed. I started to think about all of my rare experiences, as well as many experiences that can be relatable to others. I reflected on the way I think, and I noticed a trend on goals that can positively impact others—whether than through content, personal relationships, motivation, educating, charity, and overall just helping those who respect my efforts.

I began working on this book after I developed that thought, saying, "Okay, I will write a manuscript and self-publish a book before I graduate college." I rationalized the possibility of accomplishing this goal. "Would it be of benefit? How will I go about executing and making this a reality? And what will it create of me in the process?" After many deliberate conversations with myself, I took that thought and began to execute.

In order to do whatever you want to accomplish, surrounding yourself with supportive and trustworthy individuals can play a huge role in building self-trust. Associating with people who stay true to their commitments and believe in our potential can inspire confidence and provide positive reinforcement.

Impact of Winning on Social Status and Reputation

Social dynamics is another way the winning effect plays a role in our perception based on the influence it has on our social status, attraction, and interpersonal relationships. To begin with, let's look at the "social proof theory" and "mate choice copying." The social proof theory explains that when someone is unsure of how to behave in a particular situation, they tend to observe and follow the actions of others, using them as a guide for how to act. Social proof is a very powerful weapon of influence and persuasion.

Understanding the mechanisms of social proof can be greatly beneficial, as it holds significant influence and persuasion in many different areas of our lives. From consumer choices to social interactions, education, and beyond, awareness of how it works can offer valuable insights into our daily existence. Although we can use examples of marketing, entertainment, social interaction, religious practices, education, health, social causes, etc. For now, let's just focus on how it affects marketing to paint a picture.

As we know, social proof is a phenomenon where people assume the actions of others in an attempt to reflect correct behavior for a given situation. In marketing, businesses can showcase testimonials, customer reviews, endorsements from influencers, or statistics about the popularity of their product to demonstrate its value and credibility. By highlighting the positive experiences of others, potential customers are more likely to perceive the product as desirable and trustworthy, thus increasing the likelihood of purchase.

When a product is marketed using social proof, it creates a perception of success surrounding the product. By showcasing how many people are using and benefiting from the product, marketers tap into the innate desire for social acceptance and affiliation. Potential customers perceive the product as being popular and in-demand, which enhances its perceived value and attractiveness. This perception of success aligns with the winning effect, where we are drawn to entities associated with success and achievement.

The use of social proof in marketing not only influences our perceptions but also shapes social dynamics within peer groups and communities. When we see others endorsing or using a product, it can trigger a cascade effect where we feel compelled to follow suit to fit in or align with the perceived norm. This social influence further reinforces the product's success and popularity, creating a self-preserving cycle where the product becomes increasingly desirable and sought after.

Social proof can also impact perceptions of social status and identity. When people associate themselves with a successful product endorsed by others, it enhances their own perceived social status and identity. By aligning with a popular brand or product, people signal their association in a desirable social group or community, further reinforcing the positive perception of the product and contributing to its success.

Mate choice copying is a phenomenon observed in behavioral ecology, wherein a man's perceived attractiveness to certain women increases his overall appeal to a broader audience of women. This effect reinforces the role of social dynamics in shaping perceptions of attractiveness and mate selection. When women observe their peers finding a man appealing, it serves as social validation, suggesting that he possesses desirable qualities. Hence, this heightened interest not only boosts the man's confidence, but also triggers a sense of competition among potential partners and piques curiosity in others. These dynamics contribute to the perception of increased attractiveness, highlighting how social interactions influence our perceptions and the overall winning effect in mate selection. It's essential to recognize, however, that while social validation plays a role, genuine qualities such as kindness and shared values remain integral to forming meaningful relationships.

Success is built upon foundational principles that guide our decisions, interactions, and growth. The concept of choice highlights the importance of making deliberate decisions and taking ownership of one's path. By exercising choice, we align our actions with our goals and values, demonstrating confidence and intent that naturally attract opportunities. Curiosity fosters a mindset of exploration and learning, encouraging us to seek out new experiences and perspectives. In both personal and professional interactions, curiosity creates deeper engagement and connection by showing genuine interest in others' ideas and experiences. This openness to learning develops dynamic relationships and inspires innovation.

Creativity allows for innovative problem-solving and fresh perspectives. Those who approach challenges with creativity are often admired and valued for their ability to offer original ideas and solutions. This quality positions individuals as indispensable collaborators and partners. Commitment emphasizes the value of perseverance and dedication in pursuing goals. Demonstrating reliability and consistency builds trust and reinforces positive perceptions of one's character and capabilities, making it easier to build meaningful relationships and opportunities.

Compassion involves empathy and understanding, strengthening connections and promoting trust. By showing kindness and consideration for others' needs and experiences, we cultivate positive relationships that open the door to new possibilities and collaborations. Communication serves as the bridge to effectively convey ideas, build relationships, and seize opportunities. Clear and articulate communication enhances credibility and influence, allowing us to share our vision, collaborate with others, and attract meaningful opportunities.

The Winning Effect at Play in Sports, Business, and Academics

In the business world, we can use the success of a startup company as an example of the winning effect. When a tech startup develops an innovative solution and then experiences rapid growth, it leads to increased confidence among founders and employees, motivating them to innovate further and attract more investors. The startup's success is often paired with industry recognition, which enhances its credibility and opens doors to potential networking opportunities. As the startup expands, it is able to hire more 10/10s that not only are intellectually elite but also are able to adapt into the company's culture. During expansion, the startup solidifies its position in the market, and its initial success serves as a launchpad for further growth and diversification. With every success an entrepreneur has, they become more and more confident. This winning effect not only drives financial success and makes it that much easier to build the next billion dollar company, but it also encourages personal and professional development as individuals navigate the challenges of scaling a successful business.

We see this in the world of sports as well. Let's use the example of a sports team winning a championship. Following a victorious season, the team's championship win brings a surge of confidence, motivation, and unity among players and fans alike. This achievement is celebrated within the community and can lead to personal and professional benefits for individual athletes, including sponsorships and other career opportunities. Additionally, winning contributes to the team's legacy, facilitating a desire for continued excellence in future seasons and promoting personal growth among players through the challenges they overcome. The winning effect in sports encompasses emotional, psychological, and social dimensions, leaving a historical mark on the team's identity.

Three wins that you need daily to be a complete winner:

- **A physical win:** walking, running, stretching, lifting, swimming
- **A mental win:** reading, writing, creating, learning, planning
- **A spiritual win:** praying, meditating, studying, giving, growing

Potential Downsides of an Excessive Focus on Winning

We know that winning can lead to more winning; conversely, losing can lead to more losing. If things are not working out, we feel stuck and full of self-doubt. When we feel like we are losing, then we are more likely to lose, which makes us feel worse and makes things even harder. Everything is best done in moderation, and the same applies when adopting the mindset that can acknowledge and enhance the winning effect. When it comes to the winning effect, there are some challenges and limitations we must be aware of, including the potential downside of an excessive focus on winning and the risks of pressure and burnout

The opposite of the winning effect can be described as the "losing effect" or a "negative feedback loop." It occurs when we experience repeated failures or setbacks, which can lead to diminished confidence, increased stress, reduced motivation, impaired learning, a negative self-image, and potential negative effects on our biochemistry and cognitive abilities. This cycle can make it more challenging for us to succeed in future endeavors.

Life is like a highway with numerous exits leading to "Loserville." Whenever you feel tired, pressed for time, or overwhelmed, it's easy to veer off that highway. But if you stay the course, you will reach your destination as a winner. Everyone experiences challenges. But the difference between winners and losers is not in their feelings; it's in their responses. Winners don't quit or make excuses. They persevere, fueled by an unwavering perspective that views obstacles as gateways rather than roadblocks. It's remarkable what you can achieve with the relentless refusal to become fatigued or give up. If you commit to your goals and push through adversity, you will eventually attain what you desire. The only true failure comes from choosing to surrender to fear or doubt. Embracing a winner's perspective transforms challenges into opportunities for growth, propelling you toward success.

This idea of the losing effect is a very real concept because when we experience setbacks and failures, they can trigger a negative feedback loop, which becomes harder and harder to dig ourselves out of. If there is an excessive fixation on the winning effect, though, it can lead to several potential downsides that we must be aware of. Firstly, a relentless pursuit of success may result in heightened levels of stress, anxiety, and burnout. The pressure to constantly achieve and maintain a winning streak can lead to mental exhaustion and physical fatigue, overlooking overall well-being. Moreover, an excessive focus on winning may block out the importance of personal growth, learning, and holistic well-being. At times we can become so fixated on external outcomes that we neglect essential aspects of our lives, such as relationships, self-care, and emotional health. Additionally, the fear of failure and the pressure to succeed can create unrealistic expectations, leading to increased self-doubt and negative self-image. This can further lead to a cycle of anxiety and reduce confidence and resilience. While the winning effect can be a powerful motivator, it's essential to balance ambition with self-care and a healthy perspective.

Having said this, it's important to note that with the right support system, mindset, and strategies, it is possible to break this cycle and work toward success by focusing on personal growth, resilience, and a positive outlook. One way to think about the winning effect is to be aware that we are either on an upward spiral or a downward spiral. The question to ask yourself is: How much positive or negative momentum do you currently have in your life at the moment? The exciting part about the winning effect is that no matter what type of results you get, even if you have no past record of wins, the winning effect is all about perception.

"Don't think outside the box, think like there is no box."
—*Ziad K. Abdelnour*

6
WhY FiT iN?

At its core, the need to fit in originates from a hypothesized drive to form and maintain strong, stable interpersonal relationships. Researchers Baumeister and Leary (1995) argue that this "need to belong" involves frequent, non-aversive interactions within an ongoing relational bond. Throughout history, these bonds were crucial for survival, as groups provided safety, food, and resources, while isolation brought significant vulnerability. This powerful and fundamental motivation influences emotional patterns, cognitive processes, and overall well-being.[1]

Even in today's world, this primal need persists. When we feel excluded or disconnected, the emotional pain can be as intense as physical injury. Researchers Eisenberger, Lieberman, and Williams demonstrated through fMRI studies that social rejection activates the same areas of the brain associated with physical pain. This neurological response explains why fitting in feels so essential—it reassures us that we are safe and not alone. However, this drive can also compel us to sacrifice authenticity in exchange for acceptance, creating a tension between belonging to a group and remaining true to ourselves.[2]

This instinctual desire for belonging is further reinforced by a powerful fear of rejection and judgment. Denis Waitley explains that this fear begins early in life. As children, we quickly learn that standing out can result in ridicule or exclusion. A unique opinion, a bold choice, or an unconventional path often invites criticism, teaching us that it's safer to conform. Over time, these early experiences shape our behavior, pushing us toward choices that prioritize acceptance over authenticity.

Modern society magnifies this fear through constant social comparison, especially on platforms like Instagram and TikTok. Social media amplifies the human tendency to seek validation by creating environments where approval is measured in likes, comments, and followers. Researchers Chou and Edge found that individuals often perceive others as living happier and more successful lives based on curated online content. This illusion of perfection fuels insecurity and drives people to conform to societal ideals, fearing that failure to do so will result in exclusion or ridicule.[3]

The source of all insecurity is comparing your behind-the-scenes to everyone else's highlights.

The desire to fit in in often pulls us away from the guidance of our inner compass, leading us to conform to external expectations or adopt identities that don't reflect who we truly are. The pressure to belong can cloud our judgment, causing us to ignore the quiet whispers of our inner compass that are trying to guide us toward authenticity. However, when we choose to listen to our inner compass, we realize that true belonging doesn't require us to change ourselves—it requires us to align with our truest self.

Insecurity often manifests as a compulsion to keep up with others, rushing through life in a desperate attempt to meet perceived expectations. Instead of trusting their unique path, individuals feel pressure to mimic societal norms, whether in their careers, relationships, or personal appearances. This external focus erodes the confidence required to stay true to oneself, leaving people trapped in a cycle of conformity and comparison.

Ironically, while the fear of rejection often drives us to conform, this very conformity can leave us feeling profoundly empty and disconnected. Brené Brown highlights that when we "fit in" rather than truly belong, we adapt to situations by sacrificing our authenticity instead of standing for our true selves. This acclimation creates counterfeit connections, where external approval replaces genuine relationships. The cost of this conformity, as Brown notes, is the loss of personal integrity and a diminished sense of self-worth, leaving us feeling more lonely and disconnected from who we truly are.[4]

To break free from the need to fit in, we must embrace vulnerability as a core aspect of our emotional and spiritual lives. Brené Brown explains that vulnerability is not a weakness but the birthplace of love, belonging, joy, courage, and creativity. By redefining vulnerability as uncertainty, risk, and emotional exposure, we can see it as essential to meaningful connections and authentic living. As Brown notes, when we foreclose on our emotional lives out of fear of rejection or failure, we walk away from the very things that give purpose and meaning to living. True belonging requires us to risk emotional exposure and rejection—not to fit in with others, but to remain true to ourselves. Vulnerability is the path that leads us to deeper connections and a stronger sense of authenticity.

Denis Waitley emphasizes that overcoming the fear of rejection requires reframing how we interpret "no." He explains that rejection is not a reflection of personal worth but often a sign that the timing or presentation isn't right. To conquer this fear, we must separate our self-esteem from external outcomes and view rejection as an opportunity to grow. Waitley likens rejection to a waiter offering a dessert—when a patron declines, it doesn't diminish the value of the dessert or the waiter's worth. Similarly, taking risks is essential to growth, love, and success. "To place your ideas and dreams before a crowd is to risk rejection," Waitley writes, but he reminds us that "the greatest hazard in life is to risk nothing at all." True freedom and fulfillment come from embracing risks and seeing rejection as part of the journey.[5]

Understanding the roots of this drive can empower us to make conscious choices. While the need to belong may have once been essential for survival, today it often holds us back from achieving personal growth and authenticity. By acknowledging our fears and learning to trust our individual paths, we can move beyond the superficial comfort of fitting in and toward the deeper fulfillment of belonging to ourselves.

> *Loneliness is solitude. Solitude is loneliness. Your perspective determines which one you use.*

Why Is It Beneficial to Belong to Ourselves?

Belonging to ourselves—choosing authenticity over conformity—opens the door to a life of deeper, long-term fulfillment. In contrast, the comfort that comes from fitting in is often fleeting. Social acceptance may soothe the immediate discomfort of rejection, but it rarely addresses the core human need for meaning and purpose The contrast between these two paths becomes even clearer over time. The short-term benefits of fitting in—avoiding conflict, gaining approval, or meeting societal benchmarks— are often undermined by the long-term consequences of suppressing our true self. Dr. Gabor Maté, Canadian physician, emphasizes that the pain of losing oneself can manifest in both mental and physical health challenges, as the internal conflict of living inauthentically creates a ripple effect across all areas of life. Conversely, belonging to ourselves allows us to cultivate an inner peace and satisfaction that far outweighs any temporary discomfort we might face when resisting societal pressures.[6]

The journey toward authenticity is often accompanied by a period of isolation. As we grow and evolve, old relationships may no longer align

authentic   not perfect

with our values, leaving us in an interim phase where new connections have not yet formed. While this loneliness can be challenging, it ultimately leads to stronger, more meaningful relationships built on trust and mutual understanding. It's important to remember that the rewards of authenticity far outweigh the temporary discomforts of breaking free from conformity. For example, prioritizing authenticity helps build more meaningful relationships. While conformity may lead to shallow connections based on mutual agreement, living authentically attracts others who value and respect the real you. These relationships are built on a foundation of trust and mutual understanding, creating bonds that are far more fulfilling than those based on pretense.

The consequences of living inauthentically are profound. Suppressing our true selves to meet societal expectations often results in a deep, lingering dissatisfaction. This disconnection from our authentic selves can lead to feelings of shame, low self-worth, and a pervasive sense of feeling like we are not enough. Over time, the cost of denying who we truly are can take the form of strained relationships, unfulfilling careers, and a loss of purpose.

Dr. Maté also highlights the toll that inauthenticity takes on both mental and physical health. When we suppress our needs and desires to conform, we create an internal dissonance that often manifests as stress, anxiety, or even chronic illness. This internal struggle is not only exhausting but also diminishes our ability to thrive. Instead of experiencing the joy and vitality that comes from living authentically, we are weighed down by the emotional burden of pretending to be someone we're not. Many people mistakenly believe that success and happiness come from meeting societal expectations, only to find themselves trapped in a cycle of frustration and exhaustion. By living inauthentically, we lose the resilience and drive that come from staying true to our unique paths, ultimately feeling unfulfilled despite external achievements.

Social media intensifies this cost. The constant comparison fostered by platforms like Instagram creates a pressure to present an idealized version of ourselves. This curated facade may win us approval in the short term, but it only deepens the divide between who we are and who we pretend to be. Over time, this disconnect erodes our sense of identity, making it even harder to reconnect with our authentic selves.

Living authentically is not only beneficial for the individual but also for the world. When we embrace our unique qualities and perspectives, we unlock the ability to make meaningful contributions to society. Steve Jobs famously observed that the world is shaped by people no smarter than us, a realization that should inspire us to challenge the status quo and create something new. By daring to live authentically, we open the door to innovation, creativity, and impact. Motivation reinforces this idea, emphasizing that relentless effort is essential for achieving greatness. Authenticity requires a commitment to continuous self-improvement, even in the face of discomfort. This drive to constantly grow not only benefits us but also serves as an inspiration to others, demonstrating the power of perseverance and authenticity.

Take Virgil Abloh, Ghanaian-American fashion designer and entrepreneur, whose has spoken on the importance of environment. Just as the context of a candle changes its perceived value, our surroundings influence how our authenticity is received. Abloh suggests that we can either focus on designing the candle or the room it sits in—emphasizing that our value and identity can be shaped not only by who we are but by where we choose to be. By curating environments that support our individuality—whether through designing physical spaces that reflect our values, cultivating supportive relationships, or pursuing careers aligned with our purpose— we create spaces where our unique contributions can flourish.[7] This approach underscores the importance of aligning our surroundings with our true selves, making it easier to live authentically and present ourselves in the best possible light. Living authentically allows us to contribute to the world in a way that only we can, while ensuring that our individuality is respected and appreciated.

The contributions of authentic individuals often inspire others to do the same. Authenticity is contagious. When one person dares to live true to themselves, it encourages others to embrace their own uniqueness. This ripple effect creates a culture of innovation, diversity, and resilience. Whether it's an artist challenging societal norms, an entrepreneur introducing groundbreaking ideas, or a parent modeling authenticity for their children, the impact of living authentically extends far beyond the individual.

By belonging to ourselves, we tap into a wellspring of personal fulfillment, health, and meaningful contribution. Authenticity is not merely a personal virtue; it is a powerful force for societal progress, creativity, and connection. Choosing to live authentically is choosing to invest in a life of purpose and impact, rather than settling for the fleeting comfort of conformity.

7
Monk Mode
A Path to Self-Mastery

The journey of personal growth begins with the fundamental principle that we can never surpass our own self-belief. To elevate ourselves, we must first focus on self-improvement. Decide what areas of your life you want to enhance, and dedicate yourself to mastering them. By committing to self-mastery, you maximize your potential and become the best versions of yourself. This journey not only transforms you but also sets a powerful example for others, inspiring them to embark on their own paths of self-improvement. In essence, to create positive change in the world, you must first embody that change yourself. Monk mode embodies this principle by creating a structured period of intense focus and dedication to personal growth. This disciplined approach allows you to isolate yourself from distractions and commit fully to your development, thus maximizing your potential.

The Power of Isolation and Focus

Jay Shetty, author of *On Purpose*, referenced a fascinating study where men and women were asked to choose between being alone with their thoughts for fifteen minutes or giving themselves an electric shock. Surprisingly, 30 percent of women and 60 percent of men chose the electric shock over solitude. This startling result highlights our struggle with being present in our own minds, bodies, and hearts.[1] We often resort to distractions to avoid this discomfort. Shetty emphasizes the importance of developing the habit of being present with yourself, fully experiencing and reflecting on our thoughts, both when we are content and when we feel we could have done better.

Monk Mode thrives on this concept of isolation, encouraging us to embrace solitude and use it as a tool for deep introspection and personal growth. By cutting out distractions, we can better understand ourselves and our aspirations and fully live in the now. Eric Thomas, author and minister, emphasizes the need for intense focus and sacrifice to achieve one's goals. He suggests eliminating distractions such as TV, parties, and unproductive activities. For those with high academic or professional aspirations, he advises dedicating time to studying and improving skills. Thomas humorously illustrates his point by saying that if someone calls him, they should expect an unavailable message until the end of the year because he is fully committed to his goals. This level of dedication and prioritization, he argues, is crucial for success.[2] In the context of Monk Mode, this means prioritizing your goals above all else and creating an environment conducive to achieving them. This relentless focus, or "grindset," is what propels individuals toward their highest potential.

The inner compass isn't about always making "perfect" decisions but about navigating life in a way that feels deeply aligned and true to you. By learning to listen to and trust this internal guide, you can create a life of authenticity, purpose, and joy.

Alex Hormozi, entrepreneur and philanthropist, discusses the inevitable "lonely chapter" in the journey of anyone striving to achieve something significant. During this phase, you may feel out of place with your current friends and have not yet reached the outcomes that would integrate you into a new circle. You might find yourself learning from free online tutorials, questioning whether your efforts are worth it, and facing criticism from others. Hormozi warns against succumbing to this criticism and reverting to comfortable conformity. He compares this moment to a scene from *The Matrix*, where Morpheus offers Neo the choice between the red pill and the blue pill: the red pill, representing the challenging but rewarding path of truth, and the blue pill, symbolizing the safety of ignorance. Hormozi likens this to choosing whether to stay on the difficult journey of becoming who you are meant to be or retreating to the familiar but unfulfilling life.[3] Monk Mode is all about navigating this lonely chapter, using the isolation to build resilience and stay committed to your path despite external pressures.

> *"Loneliness is a kind of tax you have to pay to atone for a certain complexity of mind."* —Alain de Botton

Isolation is often a powerful tool for achieving clarity, focus, and extraordinary work. Throughout history, many great creators and thinkers have found that stepping away from the distractions of the world can lead to their most impactful achievements. Whether it's finding solace in a secluded cabin, retreating to a quiet library, or simply creating a distraction-free space, these moments of solitude allow for deep reflection, creativity, and mastery of one's craft.

Taking time to disconnect—free from the constant pull of social media and daily obligations—creates the mental space needed to enter a flow state and produce meaningful work. During these retreats, activities like meditation, prayer, visualization, reading timeless literature, or focusing intensely on a creative project can help nurture inspiration and insight. It's not about vanishing for long periods; even short, intentional breaks can be transformative. Whether it's a getaway to a new city or simply carving out time in a quiet corner, isolation can provide the perspective and environment needed to unlock your best ideas. Sometimes, stepping back is essential for stepping forward into your full potential.

How to Reconnect
with Your Inner Compass

Quiet the Noise:
Spend time in silence or mindfulness
to tune in to your inner voice.

Trust Your Feelings:
Pay attention to how situations and decisions
make you feel emotionally and physically.

Reflect on Values:
Clarify what truly matters to you to align
decisions with your core principles.

Practice Self-Awareness:
Journaling, meditation, or deep conversations
can help uncover your inner guidance.

Act on Intuition:
Start small by trusting your gut on minor decisions,
and build confidence in its accuracy.

Will Smith once emphasized that no one can truly advise you on what you should do with your life, because only you know your true potential. Sometimes, even you might not fully understand your own capabilities. You have to take your shot at your dreams, regardless of whether others agree or support you. The path to achieving your dreams is often a lonely, solitary, and dangerous pursuit. You cannot wait for others to believe in you; you must believe in yourself first. Smith underscores the importance of self-belief and the willingness to pursue your dreams even when you're alone. Initially, people may not support you, but as you make progress and gain momentum, others will start to join and support your journey. However, if you lack belief in yourself, no one else will believe in you either.[4] Pursuing your dreams requires fearlessness and relentless determination, as you must be willing to risk everything to become the person you envision.

Paul Han, famous YouTuber, spoke about his yearlong Monk-Mode journey saying it was the "best decision I've ever made." It also exemplifies this principle. He dedicated a year to intense self-improvement, cutting off distractions and committing fully to his goals.[5] By focusing on self-education and business, he achieved significant financial success. Han's extensive Monk Mode story highlights the importance of personal responsibility and the power of compound growth through consistent effort. His transformation during Monk Mode shows how self-belief and responsibility can lead to profound personal and financial growth.

Reevaluate Your Path: Choose What You Fear Most

Jensen Huang, cofounder of Nvidia, explains the rationale behind choosing incredibly difficult tasks. He argues that opting for something extremely hard to do ensures ample time for learning and growth. In contrast, if a task is easy, like playing tic-tac-toe, it wouldn't warrant much effort or be worth the competition. The inherent difficulty of a challenging task naturally deters many others, leaving only those who are truly committed. The person willing to endure the most suffering is often the one who ultimately succeeds. Huang outlines three key reasons for choosing hard goals: high competition, alignment with your unique qualities, and a passion for the work. By focusing on these principles, Huang believes that individuals can achieve the greatest success in their endeavors.[6] Monk Mode embodies Huang's philosophy by encouraging us to tackle challenging tasks that advance growth and resilience. The isolation and focus required in Monk Mode help individuals commit to these difficult goals and develop the endurance needed for success.

The Hindustan Times reveals powerful insights from Cornell psychologist Tom Gilovich, who wrote a paper in the journal *Emotion* revealing that 76 percent of people on their deathbeds regret not living life for themselves, but rather according to others' expectations. This staggering statistic suggests that over three-quarters of people realize too late that they missed out on their true desires.[7] Why it isn't this topic more widely discussed? Gilovich outlines three main reasons for this widespread regret: lack of deadlines for personal goals, waiting for inspiration, and fear of what others think or fear of failure. This issue is not new but is becoming more pronounced. The regret of not living authentically is now recognized as a major concern, emphasizing the need to create accountability, take action, and overcome fear to avoid this common regret.

What Is Stealing Your Quality Time?

A 2018 article in DailyGood states, "The destruction of our inner selves via the wired world is an even more recent, and more subtle, phenomenon. The loss of slowness, of time for reflection and contemplation, of privacy and solitude, of silence, of the ability to sit quietly in a chair for fifteen minutes without external stimulation—all have happened quickly and almost invisibly. A hundred and fifty years ago, the telephone didn't exist. Fifty years ago, the Internet didn't exist. Twenty-five years ago, Google didn't exist." We seem to be getting more and more out of touch with ourselves, losing the ability to discern what is important and giving up our control to limit our use of technology. The article goes on to say, "We are creating a global machine in which each of us is a mindless and reflexive cog, relentlessly driven by the speed, noise, and artificial urgency of the wired world."[8]

How can we stop this madness? We need to start prioritizing solitude, slowness, stillness, privacy, and make room for moments of personal reflection. When we honor our inner self, our life can drastically change for the better. If we can shift gears and unplug from the technology chatter around us, then we can experience enhanced creativity, reduced anxiety, greater confidence (because of less time playing the comparison game), a sense of well-being, and something else . . . more time!

A 2024 study found that Americans spend, on average, two hours and twenty-four minutes a day on social media. How often do we check our phones? A staggering 159 times per day! Forty-six percent of Americans say they watch more user-generated content on social media than they watch movies and television on streaming services. And Americans spend 4.2 hours per day on mobile gaming.[9]

The journey of personal growth and success requires isolation, focus, discipline, and the elimination of distractions. It demands relentless self-belief and the willingness to pursue challenging goals passionately and persistently. Surround yourself with people who inspire and challenge you, and remember that the path to achieving your dreams is often lonely and difficult. Embrace this journey, embody the change you wish to see, and inspire others by becoming the best version of yourself.

> *"People struggle to do things alone. The path of an exceptional person is one of an exception, which means that you are not with other people."* —Alex Hormozi

Monk Mode encapsulates all these principles, providing a structured approach to personal growth. By embracing solitude, focusing intensely on goals, committing to self-improvement, choosing challenging paths, and surrounding oneself with supportive and inspiring individuals, anyone can achieve profound personal and professional transformation. Adopting a "grindset" mentality and living in the now ensures that every moment is utilized for growth, paving the way for sustained success and fulfillment.

8
The Power of
Positive Self-Talk
Daily Reminders

The words we tell ourselves hold incredible power. They can shape our reality, guide our actions, and fuel our aspirations. This chapter is dedicated to the transformative practice of positive self-talk, mantras, and affirmations. These tools are more than just phrases; they are anchors in moments of doubt, sparks of inspiration during challenges, and daily reminders of who we strive to become.

Positive affirmations, when guided by our inner compass, become more than just uplifting words—they become powerful tools for alignment and self-trust. Our inner compass reveals what resonates deeply with our authentic self, and positive affirmations help reinforce that alignment by rewiring our mindset to support the path we are meant to follow.

In the following sections, you'll find curated mantras and principles designed to help you cultivate discipline, embrace resilience, and focus on growth. Whether you're looking to overcome obstacles, build self-confidence, or strengthen your sense of purpose, these phrases offer a framework for meaningful change. Use them to reframe your mindset, align your actions with your goals, and discover the profound impact of a positive inner voice.

Personal Growth and Self-Discipline

- Prove Yourself Right (PYR).
- The harder you are on yourself, the easier life will be on you.
- Gain and maintain.
- Your perspective is your reality.
- The magic you are looking for is in the work you're avoiding.
- Nothing gets easier. You must handle the hard better.
- The quality of our lives is directly proportional to the quality of questions we ask ourselves. —Quazi Johir
- Be stronger than your excuse.
- Your present self is an accumulation of your past habits and daily actions.
- Your lack of commitment is almost an insult to the people who believe in you. —Connor McGregor

- The world only rewards action.
- Smart people know what they want. Wise people know what they don't want. —Jack Ma
- You can't cheat the grind, for the grind knows what you put in.
- The greatest responsibility of your life is to be in control of your own thoughts. —Tony Robbins

Leadership and Influence

- Be a thought leader.
- Ownership is the key to freedom.
- Who you listen to is who you become.
- Success is about proximity.
- Use your unfair advantage.
- Never mistake kindness for weakness.
- People don't love you if they don't challenge you.
- Quiet confidence is powerful.
- Power follows the blame finger.
- Leadership = More humble, more kind, better listener.

Risk, Opportunity, and Success

- It's a good day to have a good day.
- Opportunity unlocks opportunity.
- Take the risk or lose the chance.
- No risk, no story.
- The biggest risk is taking no risk.
- Risk is the entry fee for greatness.
- Success is the price of sacrifice.
- Add immediate value, not the promise of future value.
- Life is not about how much you succeed but how you handle failure.
- Life takes from takers and gives to givers.

Faith, Family, and Values

- Faith, family, freedom
- God did and is still doing.
- Blessed are those who don't see and still believe.
- The fear of God is the beginning of wisdom.
- Realize what you have before you lose it.
- Never let success get to your head, and never let failure get to your heart.
- Life is good, but I want you to see that life is great.
- Love never fails, and if it does, it was never love.
- Keep your head up. The only time you head goes down is when you pray.
- Treasure you protect, and trophies you collect.

Resilience, Struggle, and Adversity

- Exhaustion makes cowards of us all. —Lex Fridman
- When you get complacent, you lose respect for winning. —Nick Saban
- Stay small enough, long enough. You'll be big enough, soon enough.
- My resilience is greater than my resistance.
- If you want to shrink your problems, grow your purpose.
- Old habits die hard.
- Everyone wants the view, but they don't want the climb. —Alex Hormozi
- Nothing changes if nothing changes.
- The rarer you are, the rarer the people who share your perspective; in this way, the greater your success, the fewer people you can share it with.
- Being realistic is the most commonly traveled road to mediocrity. —Will Smith

- Never let your emotions supersede your intelligence.
- Grateful people attract opportunities.
- If your day doesn't challenge you, then never expect to be changed by it.
- Good times don't last forever, but neither do bad times.

Learning and Wisdom

- Knowledge is the fertilizer to wealth.
- Learn who to listen to.
- Vision is the art of seeing what is invisible to others.
- Information makes you smart; experience makes you wise.
- A problem well–understood is a problem half-solved.
- Beliefs are what you think is true. Values are what you think are important.
- Actions are the manifestation of the mind.
- Kids don't do what you say; they do what you do.
- It takes wisdom to recognize wisdom.
- Make sure you fail doing exactly what you want.

Money, Wealth, and Finance

- Money is a great servant but a horrible master. —Graham Cochrane
- Money enhances your intentions.
- Price is only an issue if value is absent.
- Money is a store of value.
- Some people are so poor, all they have is money.
- Algebra of wealth = focus + stoicism x time x diversification. —Scott Galloway
- Ask for 1% of their confidence and earn the other 99%.
- Concentration builds wealth, diversification keeps it.

- One who does, wins.
- You will only scale as fast as your ability to delegate.
- The more hands you shake, the more money you make.
- Great ideas come from lots of ideas.
- It takes twenty years to build a reputation and five minutes to ruin it. —Warren Buffett

Motivation and Action

- Stay the course.
- Pressure is an illusion. It's what you make it.
- Most people don't lead their life; they accept their life.
- Make excuses or make progress.
- Forget the mistake. Remember the lesson.
- The same walls that are protecting you are the same ones blocking your blessings.
- Pain is the gatekeeper of destiny.
- Comfortability will kill success.
- When you can't stay motivated, stay consistent.
- Slow down, but don't stop.

The Power of "I Am" Statements

Words shape our thoughts, and our thoughts shape our reality. Among the most powerful tools for influencing your mindset are "I am" statements—affirmative declarations that focus on what you want to embody or achieve. Unlike phrases that dwell on avoidance or negativity, "I am" statements direct your energy toward the positive and actionable. They serve as both a reminder of who you are and a vision of who you aim to become, reinforcing your beliefs and driving your behavior in meaningful ways.

Psychologically, "I am" statements tap into the brain's ability to process self-relevant information. Studies in cognitive and behavioral psychology have shown that the language we use can strengthen neural pathways associated with confidence, motivation, and resilience. By declaring, "I am disciplined," you not only reinforce the identity of a disciplined person but also guide your actions to align with that belief. In contrast, focusing on what you don't want ("I don't want to fail ") may unintentionally emphasize fear or doubt, creating a mental hurdle.

Psychologically, affirmations work by creating new neural pathways in the brain, helping us form habits of thought that align with our goals and values. They are a tool for rewiring your mindset, pushing back against doubt, fear, or negativity, and focusing instead on growth, possibility, and confidence.

Negative Framing vs. Positive Declaration

Consider these examples of reframing a negative mindset into a positive affirmation:

- **Negative:** "I don't want to fail."
  Positive: "I am resilient and prepared to succeed."

- **Negative:** "I don't want to feel overwhelmed."
  Positive: "I am calm, focused, and capable."

- **Negative:** "I don't want to be lazy."
  Positive: "I am motivated and energized."

Shifting your language from avoidance to affirmation empowers you to see opportunities instead of obstacles and to take proactive steps toward your goals.

Examples of "I Am" Mantras

Here are a few "I am" statements for inspiration:
- I am disciplined and committed to my growth.
- I am confident in my ability to overcome challenges.
- I am grateful for the opportunities in my life.
- I am a leader who inspires and uplifts others.
- I am a creator of meaningful change.

- I am strong, capable, and focused on my purpose.
- I am becoming the best version of myself every day.

Adopting "I am" statements into your daily routine—whether spoken aloud, written down, or repeated in your thoughts—can help you reshape your perspective and align your actions with your aspirations. They are not just affirmations; they are declarations of the person you are choosing to be.

Affirmations vs. Negative Self-Talk

Negative self-talk can hold us back, creating a narrative of fear or inadequacy. Consider the difference between these two internal dialogues:

- **Negative**: "I don't think I can handle this."
  Affirmation: "I am strong, capable, and prepared to face challenges."

- **Negative**: "I'm not good enough for this opportunity."
  Affirmation: "I am worthy of success, and I embrace opportunities with confidence."

By replacing self-limiting thoughts with affirmations, you're actively choosing to focus on your strengths and potential instead of your fears.

Examples of Affirmations

Here are categorized examples of affirmations to inspire and guide your practice:

- **Personal Growth:**
  - "I am growing stronger, wiser, and more capable every day."
  - "I am in control of my thoughts and actions."
  - "I am committed to becoming the best version of myself."
- **Overcoming Challenges:**
  - "I am resilient and able to handle whatever comes my way."
  - "I am calm, focused, and resourceful in tough situations."
  - "I am learning and growing through every experience."

- Gratitude:
  - "I am grateful for the opportunities and blessings in my life."
  - "I am thankful for the lessons I've learned and the progress I've made."
  - "I am surrounded by love, support, and positivity."
- Success and Ambition:
  - "I am worthy of success, and I work diligently to achieve it."
  - "I am confident in my ability to achieve my goals."
  - "I am creating opportunities for growth and prosperity."
- Self-Love and Confidence:
  - "I am enough, just as I am."
  - "I am deserving of love, respect, and kindness."
  - "I am proud of who I am and what I am becoming."

How to Use Affirmations

Incorporating affirmations into your daily life is a practice of discipline and intention. To make the most of these powerful tools, follow these practical steps:

- **Acknowledge Them Daily:** Begin each day by focusing on your affirmations. Whether you speak them aloud, write them down, or visualize them, let them be a cornerstone of your morning routine to set a positive tone.
- **Start with Discipline and Intention:** Pair your affirmations with an action that reinforces their meaning. For example, if your affirmation is, "I am disciplined and focused," follow it by completing a task or habit that requires discipline.
- **Write Them Down or Visualize Them:** Journaling your affirmations or visualizing them in action makes them feel more tangible. Picture yourself living the truth of your affirmations, achieving goals, and embodying the traits you declare.

- **Believe Them:** Affirmations only work when you invest in them emotionally. Repeat them with conviction and believe in their truth, even if it feels unfamiliar at first. Over time, your actions will align with your words.

- **Return to Them in Times of Doubt:** During moments of challenge, uncertainty, or self-doubt, revisit your affirmations. Let them ground you and remind you of your strengths, your purpose, and your commitment to growth.

Life is a series of choices, challenges, and opportunities, and the way we speak to ourselves can define how we navigate it all. The mantras and affirmations shared in this chapter are not just words; they are tools for growth, resilience, and transformation. They remind us that our thoughts shape our actions, and our actions shape our future. From mastering discipline and embracing resilience to seeking balance and cultivating gratitude, these mantras guide us to live with intention and clarity. They encourage us to face challenges with courage, celebrate progress with humility, and remain steadfast in our pursuit of a meaningful life.

As you adopt these principles into your daily routine, remember that each affirmation is a step toward the person you're striving to become. Let these words inspire you, motivate you, and ground you in the belief that you have the power to transform your life. The journey to greatness starts with a single thought, so make it a positive one.

9
Silent Thieves
How Distractions Steal Your Success

In your quest to become the best version of yourself, one of the most formidable challenges you will face is mastering the art of identifying and eliminating the countless distractions that constantly vie for your attention. These distractions are omnipresent, whether you're navigating the hallways of a school, the social dynamics of college life, or the responsibilities of adulthood. Yet the ability to filter out the unnecessary noise and focus on your true goals is what sets the truly successful apart from the rest.

The key to achieving your goals lies not just in recognizing distractions but in being intentional about how you allocate your time and energy. Successful individuals consciously choose to focus on what truly matters, limiting distractions to the unavoidable. However, this requires a significant shift in perspective—a shift that allows you to see beyond the immediate gratification of indulgence and focus on the long-term impact of your choices. Distractions may appear harmless at first glance, but their costs are often hidden in plain sight.

Distractions can easily pull us away from the guidance of our inner compass, leaving us feeling scattered, unfulfilled, or off-course. In a world filled with endless demands, noise, and external influences, it's easy to lose sight of what truly matters. However, by tuning into our inner compass, we can navigate distractions with clarity and purpose, staying aligned with our authentic path.

Take college life, for instance. Distractions often come in the form of parties, social pressures, and the allure of activities that, while seemingly harmless, can lead to wasted time and diminished well-being. Engaging in excessive drinking may feel like a rite of passage, but it often results in hangovers that rob you of time and energy—precious resources that could be better spent pursuing your aspirations. These indulgences create an illusion of instant gratification, but they drain your energy, erode self-discipline, and generate inertia that is difficult to overcome. Each hour lost to recovery from these distractions is an hour that could have been spent advancing toward your goals, leading to missed opportunities and diminished momentum.

Over time, these choices compound, making it harder to get back on track, requiring even greater effort to regain lost ground. The time and energy wasted in the pursuit of short-term pleasures don't just impact personal progress; they also have ripple effects on your relationships and professional networks, limiting access to the people and opportunities that could support your growth. In essence, these distractions impose a hidden

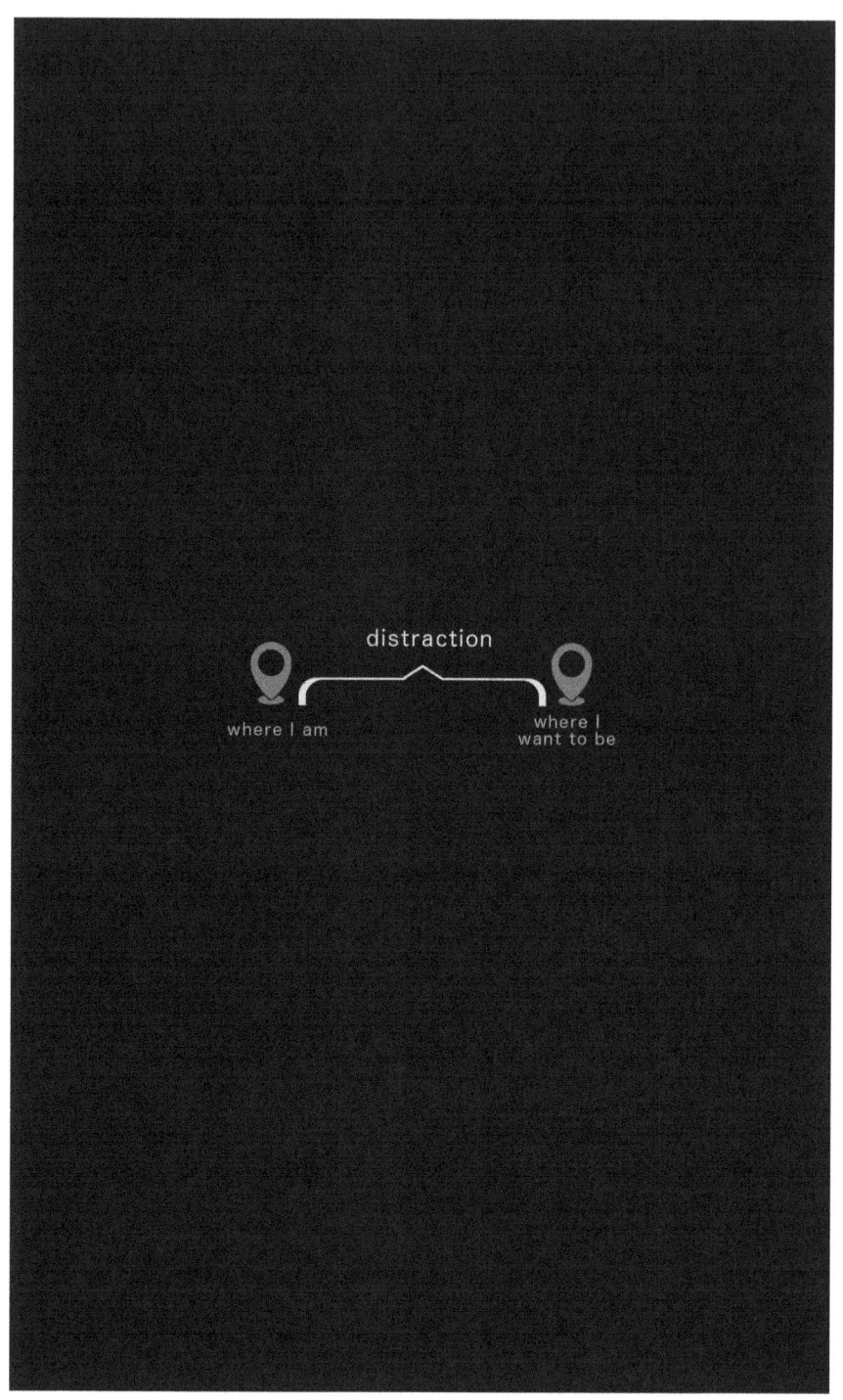

distraction

where I am

where I
want to be

cost on your potential, setting you further from your goals each time you indulge in them.

The social landscape of your life also plays a significant role in the distractions you face. The old adage, "You become the sum of your closest five friends," underscores the profound impact of your inner circle. The habits, mindsets, and attitudes of those around you inevitably shape your own. If you're surrounded by individuals who align with your goals and inspire you to grow, you are more likely to stay focused on your vision. Conversely, if your circle encourages behaviors or distractions that detract from your goals, they will hold you back. In today's hyper-connected world, this influence extends to the digital realm. Social media, in particular, has become one of the most pervasive distractions, instilling a culture of comparison that leads to overthinking and insecurity. The constant barrage of curated content can easily derail your focus, making it difficult to stay attuned to your objectives.

If you don't separate yourself from distractions, your distractions will separate you from your goals.

Adding to this complexity is the illusion of convenience, which often disguises itself as progress. While modern tools like smartphones can be incredibly useful, they are also designed to capture your attention and encourage immediate gratification. When something is convenient, we tend to do more of it, even if it's not beneficial in the long run. Social media notifications, for example, may feel rewarding in the moment, but they often pull us away from deeper, more meaningful work. To counteract this, you must be intentional about how you spend your time and energy, prioritizing activities that contribute to your long-term goals over short-term comforts. This might mean sacrificing some immediate ease for the greater reward of future success, but the outcome will always be worth it.

Ultimately, distractions like social media not only consume your time but also prevent you from gaining clarity about your true aspirations. The endless scrolling, likes, and comments might entertain you momentarily, but they cloud your ability to reflect on who you are and what you genuinely want to achieve. Stepping away from these distractions, even temporarily, creates the space needed for self-reflection and personal growth. It's a challenging but necessary step to realign with your purpose and regain control over your focus.

The cost of distractions goes beyond the moments they steal; they also rob you of progress, clarity, and the momentum needed to achieve your dreams. By recognizing their true impact and taking deliberate steps to limit their hold on your life, you can reclaim your energy and channel it toward what truly matters. The ability to overcome distractions and maintain focus is not just a skill but a discipline that separates those who merely dream from those who achieve. In the end, your success will hinge on your willingness to identify distractions, accept their cost, and choose to rise above them in pursuit of your goals.

The Influence of Your Environment

Your environment plays a critical role in shaping your mindset, habits, and overall success. From the people you surround yourself with to the physical and mental spaces you inhabit, every aspect of your environment exerts an influence on your journey toward self-improvement and growth. Understanding and intentionally shaping your environment can be the most powerful step you take toward reaching your full potential.

One of the most significant aspects of your environment is your social circle. Brian Tracy, author and motivational speaker, references a study by Dr. David McClelland at Harvard, which found that up to 95 percent of your success is determined by your reference group—the people you spend the most time with. These individuals unconsciously shape your attitudes, opinions, and behaviors. Surrounding yourself with positive, successful, and driven people naturally inspires you to adopt their habits and mindset, leading to your own growth and success.[1]

This principle also applies when striving to improve in specific areas of your life. Just as running with faster people makes you faster, spending time with those who excel in the areas you want to grow in will naturally pull you up to their level. However, this requires careful evaluation of your social circle. When people treat you like an option, it's essential to leave them as a choice. Trust is the cornerstone of any relationship, and when it's broken, it alters the dynamics forever. Growth often requires making tough decisions about who remains in your life, ensuring that your closest relationships align with your values and goals.

Relationships are not just about support. They can also serve as mirrors, reflecting your own aspirations and limitations. When nurtured with the right people, relationships can lift you and provide the support you need to achieve your goals. However, it's also important to recognize when certain relationships are no longer beneficial, or even harmful. It's not about rejecting people out of spite; it's about understanding that some connections may no longer serve your higher self. Letting go of these relationships with love allows you to move forward unencumbered, making room for new, more supportive connections. Trust is the foundation of any relationship. When trust is broken, it changes the nature of the relationship permanently. Sometimes, the changes we experience force us to reevaluate who we keep close. Growth often requires making difficult choices about the people we allow into our lives, ensuring that those who remain are aligned with our values and goals.

Suffering is often seen as something to be avoided, but David Goggins, retired Navy SEAL and author of *Can't Hurt Me*, suggests that on the other side of suffering is a life that many people don't even know exists. Goggins's concept of the 40 percent rule suggests that most people only push themselves to 40 percent of their potential because their brains keep them in a comfortable box. However, outside of this box—on the other side of suffering—lies endless opportunity. This idea highlights the importance of embracing discomfort and pushing beyond your perceived limits.[2] While it's natural to want to stay within the confines of what's comfortable and familiar, true growth occurs when you step outside of this comfort zone. By facing challenges head-on and embracing the discomfort that comes with growth, you can unlock new levels of potential and achievement.

To make room for new opportunities and growth, it's often necessary to let go of old habits, relationships, or beliefs that no longer serve you. Shi Heng Yi, Shaolin master and martial arts teacher, explains that for something new to come into your life, something old must go.[3] This process of letting go can be difficult, but it's essential for personal development. By releasing what no longer serves you, space is created for new experiences and opportunities that align with your goals. This idea is particularly relevant when it comes to letting go of toxic relationships or unproductive habits. While it may be difficult, it's necessary for your growth and well-being. By freeing yourself from these negative influences, you can focus on your development and move closer to your goals.

Mastering Focus and Self-Awareness

In a world filled with distractions and competing priorities, the ability to channel your energy toward meaningful goals and maintain a strong sense of self-awareness is what distinguishes the truly accomplished from the merely busy. This mastery begins with intentional goal-setting and extends to cultivating a disciplined routine, practicing mindfulness, and learning to filter out distractions that pull you away from your purpose.

A key strategy for mastering focus is setting clear, achievable goals. Rather than spreading yourself thin across multiple ambitions, it is far more effective to concentrate on a few core objectives. These objectives may include financial, physical, and purpose-driven goals. By narrowing your focus, you can dedicate more energy and resources to each goal, increasing your likelihood of success. Achieving these goals often creates a ripple effect, positively influencing other areas of your life. Jesse Itzler, author and cofounder of Marquis Jet, illustrates this principle by breaking his life down into four key areas: business, family, wellness, and relationships. He believes that if an activity doesn't contribute to progress in one of these areas, it's a waste of time.[4] This disciplined approach ensures that every action aligns with larger objectives, keeping distractions at bay.

"Your focus determines your reality." —George Lucas

Equally essential to mastering focus is the development of self-awareness— the ability to understand your thoughts, habits, and motivations. Self-awareness is the cornerstone of success because it provides the clarity needed to initiate change. Without self-awareness, it is impossible to accurately assess where you are, identify what's holding you back, or determine what needs to change for you to move forward. Developing this self-awareness allows you to eliminate unproductive habits, set clear goals, and stay aligned with your values and vision. However, cultivating self-awareness is not always easy in today's noisy world. With constant notifications, endless scrolling, and external pressures, it's easy to lose touch with your inner voice. Many people spend so much time reacting to the demands of the outside world that they fail to truly listen to themselves. To succeed, you need to quiet the external noise and tune into your internal guidance.

Comedian Kevin Hart discusses the challenge of growth and how it can create friction in relationships. He explains that growth occurs on different levels, and not everyone will understand or accept the changes you make to better yourself. Some friends may struggle to process why you choose to stop engaging in certain behaviors, especially if those behaviors were once a shared bond. Hart points out that, instead of support, you may encounter resistance or even ridicule. He describes how friends might dismiss your growth, using negativity or guilt to make you feel bad about your decision to change.[5] Progression requires you to prioritize what's best for your future, even if it means distancing yourself from habits or people who no longer align with your goals. While growth often comes with negativity from those who don't share your vision, it's ultimately about evolving toward a version of yourself that serves your higher purpose. This perspective underscores the courage and conviction needed to stay the course, even when faced with external doubts or criticism.

In an age where attention is a commodity, controlling where you direct your focus has become more important than ever. The modern media environment is designed to overwhelm and distract, with every platform competing for your time. The media environment is designed to overwhelm you and capitalize on every second of your time. Your mental brain space is still up for grabs, and if you don't take control of it, others will. Your attention is your freedom, and in a world where information is power, controlling your attention is crucial for success.

Jeff Bezos warns of the danger of convenience when it comes to attention. Tools like smartphones, while incredibly useful, often serve as attention-shortening devices. The constant stream of notifications, likes, and short-term rewards conditions us to seek immediate gratification, leaving us feeling empty and unfulfilled. To break free from this cycle, it's important to be mindful of how you use these tools and to prioritize activities that contribute to your long-term goals and well-being.

The importance of saying no to distractions, even when it means disappointing others, is a key lesson on the path to success. It often requires turning down invitations or requests that don't align with your goals, even if it upsets others. Success is frequently described as a less crowded road compared to mediocrity, as many settle for what's comfortable rather than striving for greatness. The journey to success can be compared to a turbulent plane ride, where the bumpiest moments occur during takeoff.

However, once you reach a stable cruising altitude, the turbulence lessens. If challenges arise even at that altitude, the solution is to climb higher. While mediocrity is filled with those unwilling to leave their comfort zones, greatness exists at a higher level where fewer are willing to go.

This perspective underscores that success often requires making difficult choices about time and energy—declining social invitations, avoiding unnecessary commitments, and saying no to opportunities that don't align with your vision. By prioritizing long-term goals over immediate gratification, you create space for what truly matters, ensuring your time and effort are directed toward your purpose. This disciplined approach not only sharpens your focus but also reinforces the boundaries needed to maintain clarity and progress in both your personal and professional lives.

Being present in the moment is another powerful skill that enhances both focus and self-awareness. Michael Jordan exemplified this principle through his extraordinary presence on the court. His ability to stay completely focused on the task at hand, without letting distractions or doubts cloud his mind, was a defining factor in his success. Many people struggle with being present because they are either dwelling on the past or worrying about the future. The constant mental noise prevents them from fully engaging in the present moment, where true success and fulfillment are found.

To cultivate this presence, it's important to practice mindfulness and avoid getting caught up in distractions that pull you away from the here and now. The convenience of modern tools, while helpful, can foster distraction by conditioning us to seek immediate gratification through a constant stream of notifications, likes, and short-term rewards. Overcoming this requires mindfulness in how time and energy are spent, choosing activities that contribute to long-term goals rather than indulging in short-term comfort.

Mastering focus and self-awareness requires not only the ability to eliminate distractions but also the cultivation of habits that support long-term success. Establishing a consistent routine is essential for making meaningful changes in perspective and staying on track. A well-structured routine acts as an anchor, helping you avoid distractions and maintain focus on the habits and goals that truly matter. By integrating intentional practices into your daily life, you create the structure needed to minimize external noise, maximize productivity, and stay aligned with your purpose.

Reframing Distractions as Opportunities for Growth

Distractions are often perceived as obstacles, but with the right mindset, they can be reframed as opportunities for growth and self-discovery. By learning to navigate and manage distractions effectively, you can transform them into turning points on your journey toward success. This process requires observing without absorbing, avoiding overthinking, managing stress, and maintaining a strong perspective and mindset.

One of the most important skills in dealing with distractions is learning to observe negative energy without absorbing it. As you work toward your goals, you will inevitably encounter negativity from others, whether in the form of doubt, criticism, or unhelpful attitudes. It's easy to get caught up in this energy, allowing it to lower your focus and derail your progress. Instead, practice observing these influences from a distance, recognizing them for what they are without letting them affect your state of mind. Releasing attachments to negativity—whether from relationships, situations, or thought patterns—can create the clarity and space needed for growth. By letting go of these influences with understanding and compassion, you free yourself to focus on personal development and move closer to your goals with renewed energy and purpose.

Distractions often thrive on our desire for comfort, but as David Goggins suggests, true growth occurs on the other side of discomfort. Goggins's concept of the 40 percent rule posits that most people only push themselves to 40 percent of their potential because their brains prioritize staying in a comfortable box. However, outside of this box—on the other side of suffering—lies endless opportunity. This idea highlights the importance of embracing discomfort and pushing beyond your perceived limits.[6] While it's natural to want to stay within the confines of what's comfortable and familiar, true growth occurs when you step outside of this comfort zone. By facing challenges head-on and embracing the discomfort that comes with growth, you can unlock new levels of potential and achievement.

Overthinking is a common distraction that can prevent you from taking action and achieving your goals. Dr. John Delony, host of *The John Deloney Show*, discusses the concept of the fundamental attribution error, which is the tendency to make assumptions about why others behave the way they do. This habit of getting inside someone else's head is a complete waste of time, because you'll never truly know their motives. Instead, it's better to focus on what you can control: your actions and decisions. Overthinking wastes time and creates unnecessary stress and anxiety. By learning to take things at face value and avoid overanalyzing, you can free up mental energy to focus on what really matters.[7] This shift in perspective can help you stay calm, make better decisions, and maintain your focus on your goals.

Stress can also become a major distraction, but it also offers a powerful lesson in resilience. Stress is an inevitable part of life, but how we manage it can make all the difference. Robert Sapolsky, author of *Why Zebras Don't Get Ulcers*, explains how zebras experience intense stress when fleeing from predators, but quickly return to a calm state once the threat is gone. Humans, on the other hand, often remain in a heightened state of stress long after the immediate danger has passed, worrying about future threats or ruminating on past events.[8]

This chronic stress can have severe negative impacts on our health, making it harder to achieve our goals. The lesson here is to learn how to manage stress effectively, similar to how zebras do. This involves recognizing when stress is necessary and when it's not, allowing yourself to return to a state of calm when the threat has passed. Techniques like breathwork can help manage stress, shifting your body from a high-stress state to a more relaxed, parasympathetic mode. This not only improves your mental health but also enhances your physical performance, making it easier to stay focused and productive.

Maintaining the right mindset and perspective is essential in navigating through distractions and challenges on the path to success. The way we perceive obstacles—whether as insurmountable roadblocks or opportunities for growth—often determines the outcomes we achieve. Believing in your ability to overcome challenges and staying committed to your vision builds resilience, helping you emerge stronger and more focused.

This perspective is particularly relevant when choosing who you surround yourself with. Kobe Bryant's unwavering commitment to success exemplifies this principle. He emphasized the importance of surrounding yourself with people who align with your energy and purpose. Working alongside driven and focused individuals naturally elevates your performance, whereas associating with those who lack purpose can dilute your drive and momentum. By carefully curating your inner circle, you create an environment that supports your goals, helping you navigate distractions with clarity and intent.

The mindset of success isn't about avoiding difficulties; it's about reframing them. Challenges become opportunities to learn, and setbacks are viewed as enablers rather than failures. This shift in perspective enables you to stay locked in on your goals, even when distractions threaten to pull you off course. When you focus on what truly matters, distractions lose their power, and you're able to navigate life's complexities with greater purpose and determination.

Aligning Action with Purpose

Purpose serves as a compass, steering you toward your long-term vision and providing clarity when faced with choices that could lead you astray. When your purpose is strong, it becomes a filter through which you assess the value of every action, opportunity, and relationship, making it easier to recognize and eliminate distractions that don't align with your ultimate objectives.

Purpose is not just about knowing where you want to go; it's about understanding why you're going there. This deeper connection to your "why" imbues your decisions with meaning and helps you maintain discipline, even when distractions tempt you to veer off course. For instance, a strong purpose can empower you to say no to time-wasting activities or people who don't contribute to your growth. Instead of succumbing to fleeting gratification, you're able to focus on what truly matters, using your purpose as an anchor in moments of uncertainty. This alignment ensures that your actions consistently lead you closer to your goals.

Removing distractions requires more than just willpower; it requires a clear understanding of what you're working toward. When you're unsure of your purpose, it's easy to fall into the trap of engaging in activities that feel productive but ultimately lead nowhere. Without a strong sense of direction, distractions can masquerade as opportunities, pulling you further away from your goals. Purpose provides the clarity needed to distinguish between what adds value to your life and what merely consumes your time.

Letting go of habits, people, or situations that no longer serve you can be difficult, but purpose gives you the strength and motivation to make those tough decisions. Every moment spent on distractions is a moment taken away from what truly matters. This perspective shift helps you see the cost of distractions not just in terms of time but in terms of lost progress toward your larger vision. For example, a young professional focused solely on climbing the corporate ladder may find himself burned out, with stress and poor health overshadowing financial success. By reconnecting with his purpose and setting boundaries, he can balance professional achievement with personal well-being, making meaningful progress in every area of life.

Time spent on distractions is time stolen from your potential.

A clear purpose also transforms the way you view challenges and setbacks. Instead of seeing distractions as obstacles, you begin to view them as opportunities to reaffirm your commitment to your goals. Each time you successfully move past a distraction, you reinforce your alignment with your purpose and build resilience. This process not only keeps you on track but also strengthens your ability to handle future distractions with greater ease.

The pursuit of success often brings with it the temptation to fixate on financial goals, but true fulfillment comes from a deeper sense of purpose. While money is important, it's not the most valuable thing in life. If given the choice between money and something more meaningful—like time, health, or relationships—most people would choose the latter. This perspective encourages you to focus on what truly matters in life. While financial success is important, it should not come at the expense of your health, relationships, or personal fulfillment. This balance between financial success and personal well-being becomes even more evident when considering the cost of neglecting your health and time in the relentless pursuit of wealth. One of the most fundamental lessons in life is understanding that health and time are far more valuable than money.

Chasing fulfillment—whether in relationships, health, or personal growth—often brings financial success as a byproduct. When your priorities are driven by purpose rather than profit, you create a more sustainable and rewarding path. Ask yourself: Are your current financial goals supporting your well-being and values, or are they pulling you further from them? The answer can be a powerful tool for realignment.

Ever heard of the Red Car Theory? It's a metaphorical concept that illustrates how opportunities are often right in front of us, but we fail to see them because we're not looking. If you were promised a reward for noticing every red car on your commute, you would suddenly become hyper-aware of them. The same applies to opportunities in life. If you wake up each day with the mindset of seeking opportunities, you'll start to see them everywhere. Conversely, if you're not actively looking for them, you'll miss out, even if they're right under your nose. This theory emphasizes the importance of being proactive and vigilant in pursuing your goals. Opportunities are abundant, but they require a shift in perspective to be recognized and seized.

10
The Art of Visualization
See It. Touch It. Obtain It.

Visualization isn't just about imagining success; it's about mapping out a clear path to your goals. Think of your ambitions as a destination on a GPS. Then tap into the compass within to help you visualize where you want to go. In doing so, a "dotted line" appears, showing the steps needed to get there. This metaphorical line represents the process of turning dreams into reality and guiding you through the necessary actions. The power of perspective comes into play here, too, because how you view your journey can either illuminate this path or obscure it. The more precisely you define your goals, the clearer that path becomes, leading you directly to success.

This dotted line is more than just a metaphor, though; it's a reflection of your inner clarity. When you set a goal and commit to it, your subconscious mind begins to align your actions with your desires. This is where visualization becomes crucial. By regularly picturing your desired outcome, you reinforce that dotted line, making it more vivid and easier to follow. This clarity isn't just a mental exercise; it's a practical tool that influences your decisions, your focus, and, ultimately, your success.

However, the journey isn't always straightforward. There will be detours, obstacles, and distractions along the way. How you interpret these challenges can either strengthen your resolve or lead you astray. If you see obstacles as opportunities to learn and grow, they become part of your journey rather than barriers. Visualization can be a powerful tool for connecting with and enhancing your ability to listen to your inner compass. By creating mental images of desired outcomes, peaceful states, or intuitive guidance, you can bridge the gap between your conscious mind and your inner wisdom.

The Magic Glasses: Seeing Reality As It Is

Actor and comedian Dick Gregory introduced the metaphor of the "magic glasses" to illustrate the transformative power of perspective. Once you put on these glasses, you see things as they truly are and not as you wish they were. This shift in perspective is both powerful and irreversible. Once you recognize your potential and the opportunities around you, you can't return to ignorance. This new perspective forces you to act on what you've seen, or visualized. The challenge isn't just in recognizing your potential but in embracing the responsibility that comes with it. Once your inner compass guides you toward your ideal vision, you are compelled to pursue your goals with conviction, knowing that turning back is no longer an option.

For example, consider someone at work who has always undervalued their own contributions, assuming they're just "doing their job." One day, after receiving genuine praise from a mentor or reflecting on a major project they successfully led, they put on the "magic glasses" and can finally see their worth. They realize their unique skills and potential, which inspires them to take on bigger challenges, advocate for a promotion, or even start their own business. This newfound clarity empowers them to take confident steps toward a brighter future.

The magic glasses metaphor also speaks to the isolation that can accompany personal growth. When you begin to see the world more clearly, you may find that others around you are still stuck in their old ways of thinking. This can create a sense of separation, but it's crucial to remember that your journey is your own. You can't force others to see what you see, but you can lead by example. By staying true to your vision, you might inspire others to put on their own "magic glasses" and join you on the path to self-discovery and achievement.

This perspective shift also changes how you approach challenges and setbacks. When you see things as they truly are, you are better equipped to handle adversity. You understand that failure is not the end but a part of the process. This realization allows you to persevere with confidence, knowing that each setback is an opportunity to learn and grow. The magic glasses provide the courage to keep moving forward, even when the road ahead is uncertain.

Expanding Your Mind: No Going Back

When the mind is exposed to new ideas, it undergoes a transformation that cannot be undone. This concept is closely tied to the power of perspective. When you discover your purpose—whether it's to create, educate, innovate, or inspire—you gain a new way of seeing the world. Every skill you acquire, every piece of knowledge you gain becomes a part of your expanded perspective. Even if you lose material things, your new perspective and expanded mind remain. This realization frees you from the fear of failure, as you understand that you can always rebuild, often with greater ease and insight. The only barrier to recreating success is your perspective on what's possible.

This expanded mindset is both a gift and a responsibility. It propels you forward, but it also demands that you continue to grow and pursue your potential. Once you've tasted what it's like to think bigger, to dream beyond your current circumstances, you can't go back to a limited mindset. This expansion creates a hunger for more knowledge, more experiences, and more growth. It drives you to seek out new challenges and opportunities, knowing that each one will further expand your mind and your potential.

However, this growth can also be uncomfortable. As you expand your mind, you may outgrow certain relationships, habits, or environments. This can create tension as you navigate the gap between your old life and your new mindset. It's important to recognize this as a natural part of the growth process. Embracing this discomfort is essential for continued expansion. By letting go of what no longer serves you, you create space for new opportunities that align with your expanded perspective.

Intellectual Curiosity: The Root of All Growth

At the core of personal and professional growth lies intellectual curiosity. It's the foundation upon which all success is built. Intellectual curiosity challenges you to ask, "How big can I think?" This question forces you to expand your perspective, to look beyond what's immediately in front of you and to consider the larger picture. Wanting to achieve something is one thing, but believing that you will is what truly changes the game. The shift from "want" to "will" is a shift in perspective—from a passive hope to an active belief. This change in mindset is the first step in turning curiosity into concrete achievements.

Intellectual curiosity is the driving force behind innovation and creativity. It's what pushes you to explore new ideas, to question the status quo, and to seek out new experiences. This curiosity is not just about acquiring knowledge; it's about applying that knowledge in ways that create value and drive progress. It's the spark that ignites your passion and fuels your pursuit of excellence. But intellectual curiosity also requires courage. It takes courage to ask big questions, to challenge your own assumptions, and to venture into the unknown. This courage is rooted in the belief that you have the capacity to grow, to learn, and to adapt. It's this belief that transforms curiosity from a passive interest into an active pursuit.

The Power of Language: From Want to Will

Language shapes our reality in profound ways. The words we use to describe our goals reflect our mindset and influence our actions. Since I was thirteen years old, I've kept a notebook filled with quotes that have shaped my perspective, and one principle stands out: the power of language in goal-setting. Saying, "I want to be successful," is very different from saying, "I will be successful." The first is a wish; the second is a declaration. This small shift in language changes your perspective from uncertainty to determination. It's a simple but powerful tool in reshaping how you approach your goals. This shift from *want* to *will* is more than just semantics; it's a reflection of your commitment to your goals. When you say, "I will," you're making a promise to yourself. You're declaring that success is not just a possibility but an inevitability. When you believe that success is inevitable, you're more likely to take the necessary steps to make it a reality.

The power of language extends beyond goal-setting. It influences how you perceive challenges, how you interact with others, and how you see yourself. By consciously choosing your words, you can shift your perspective and create a more positive and empowering reality. This is not about ignoring difficulties or pretending that everything is perfect. It's about framing your experiences in a way that empowers you to take control of your life and pursue your goals with confidence.

Visualization: Clarity in the Details

Once you shift your language from *want* to *will*, the next step is to visualize your goals with crystal-clear specificity. Visualization is more than just seeing a vague image of success; it's about creating a detailed mental blueprint of your future. For instance, if your goal is to buy a house, don't just visualize the idea of a house. Instead, see every detail. What does it look like? Where is it located? How does it make you feel? This level of detail sharpens your perspective, making the goal feel more real and attainable. The clearer the picture, the more likely you are to make it a reality.

"Clarity precedes success." —*Robin Sharma*

The practice of visualization goes beyond just picturing the end result. It involves visualizing the steps needed to get there, the challenges you might face, and the solutions you'll implement. This comprehensive approach to visualization prepares you mentally and emotionally for the journey ahead. It helps you anticipate obstacles and develop strategies to overcome them. By visualizing both the journey and the destination, you strengthen your resolve and increase your chances of success.

This process of detailed visualization also enhances your problem-solving abilities. When you take the time to visualize the steps toward your goal, you're more likely to spot potential challenges and come up with creative solutions. This proactive approach not only helps you stay on track but also boosts your confidence. You're no longer just hoping for success; you're actively planning for it, and this shift in perspective makes all the difference.

Creating Your Reality

The idea that we are creators of our own reality through our thoughts and words is a powerful perspective on visualization. This approach emphasizes how belief shapes the way we experience and interact with the world. By consciously choosing positive and empowering thoughts and language, it's possible to reshape your mindset and, consequently, your reality. When you adopt a perspective centered on creation and possibility, you open the door to manifesting the life you truly desire.

> *We paint our world with our thoughts*
> *and level of self-belief.*

We are not passive recipients of life's circumstances but active participants in creating our reality. This mindset shift is empowering because it places the responsibility for our success in our own hands. It encourages us to take ownership of our thoughts, our words, and our actions. By doing so, we align our inner world with our outer reality, creating a powerful synergy that drives us toward our goals.

To create the life you desire, you must first become aware of the thoughts and beliefs that shape your current reality. This requires honest self-reflection and a willingness to confront any limiting beliefs or negative thought patterns. Once you've identified these, you can begin the process of consciously choosing more empowering thoughts and beliefs.

Turning Vision into Action

Brian Tracy, a well-known author on personal development, suggests a practical exercise: Take a major goal and ask yourself, "How can I achieve this?" Then, write down twenty answers. This exercise forces you to think deeply and creatively, shifting your perspective from wishful thinking to actionable steps.[1] It's not just about having a goal; it's about engaging with that goal in a way that brings it closer to reality. This shift in perspective turns visualization from a passive activity into a powerful, active tool for success. By framing your goal as a question, you invite your mind to explore possibilities and solutions. This shift transforms your goal from a distant dream into a tangible reality. Each answer you write down brings you one step closer to achieving your goal. This process also helps you develop a roadmap for success, making the journey more manageable and less overwhelming.

> *"Success is 80% psychology and 20% strategy."*
> —*Tony Robbins*

When you put your thoughts on paper, you give them form and structure. This helps clarify your thinking and makes your goals more concrete. It also serves as a reference point that you can revisit and refine as you progress. This exercise is not just about generating ideas; it's about creating a clear and actionable plan that guides your efforts and keeps you focused on your goal.

Making Success Tangible Through Visualization

Visualization isn't just about daydreaming; it's a practice that aligns your thoughts with your desired outcomes. Before a big presentation, exam, or personal milestone, take time to visualize your success in vivid detail. Israel "The Last Stylebender" Adesanya, a UFC champion, attributes much of his success to visualization, where he not only sees himself winning, but dominating. This practice strengthens your perspective, making success feel tangible and within reach. By regularly visualizing your goals, you train your mind to see them as achievable, which naturally influences your actions toward making them a reality.

Visualization engages both your conscious and subconscious mind. When you vividly imagine a successful outcome, your brain begins to act as if that outcome is already happening. This creates a sense of familiarity and confidence, which can significantly enhance your performance. By visualizing success repeatedly, you condition your mind to expect it, making it easier to achieve in reality.

This practice also has a profound impact on your emotional state. When you visualize yourself succeeding, you experience the positive emotions associated with that success: joy, pride, satisfaction. These emotions create a positive feedback loop, reinforcing your belief in your ability to achieve your goals. This shift in perspective from doubt to confidence can be the difference between success and failure. By making success tangible in your mind, you make it more attainable in reality.

Repetition: Building Confidence Through Practice

Confidence often comes from repetition. When you repeat an action, whether it's studying, practicing a skill, or training physically, you build a foundation of confidence. This repetition solidifies your perspective on what you're capable of achieving. When you repeat a task or skill, you deepen your understanding and enhance your ability to perform it effortlessly. This process of repetition builds muscle memory and mental resilience, making it easier to perform under pressure.

This practice also reinforces your commitment to your goals. Each time you repeat an action, you're investing in your success. This consistent effort creates a sense of momentum, making it easier to stay focused and motivated. Over time, this repetition transforms your perspective, helping you see challenges as opportunities for growth rather than obstacles to be feared. By embracing repetition, you lay the groundwork for long-term success and continuous improvement.

Visualization and the Brain

Deepak Chopra's research reveals that the brain doesn't distinguish between an actual experience and an imagined one. This means that when you visualize success, your brain reacts as if you're already succeeding, reinforcing that perspective. If you imagine a stressful event, your body responds with stress hormones; if you visualize a positive outcome, your body responds positively.[2] This insight highlights the power of perspective. What you choose to focus on can directly impact your physical and emotional state. By consciously visualizing success, you align your body and mind with that success, making it more likely to occur.

> "What you think, you become. What you feel, you attract.
> What you imagine, you create." —the Buddha

Chopra's insights reveal the physiological effects of visualization. When you vividly imagine a successful outcome, your brain releases the same chemicals and activates the same neural pathways as if you were actually experiencing that success. This creates a powerful mind-body connection that can enhance your performance and well-being. By visualizing success regularly, you can condition your body to respond positively to challenges, reducing stress and increasing resilience.

This understanding of the mind-body connection also emphasizes the importance of managing your thoughts and emotions. By consciously choosing to focus on positive outcomes, you can influence your body's response to stress and adversity. This shift in perspective empowers you to take control of your mental and physical health, creating a more balanced and fulfilling life. Visualization is not just a mental exercise; it's a holistic practice that can transform your entire being.

Manifestation: Turning Thoughts into Reality

Manifestation is the art of turning thoughts into reality through focused intention and belief. Conor McGregor, a world-renowned MMA fighter, believes that if you have a clear picture in your head of what you want, it will happen. This perspective is shared by many successful individuals who understand that the power of belief, combined with action, creates tangible results. Manifestation isn't just wishful thinking. It's about aligning your perspective, words, and actions with your goals, making success an inevitable outcome.

Manifestation requires more than just positive thinking; it demands action and persistence. To manifest your desires, you must first believe that they are possible, then take consistent steps toward making them a reality. This process involves setting clear intentions, visualizing your success, and aligning your actions with your goals. By doing so, you create a powerful synergy between your thoughts and actions, which propels you toward your desired outcome.

This practice also involves letting go of doubt and fear. Manifestation requires a deep sense of trust in yourself and the universe. It's about believing that you have the power to create your reality, even in the face of obstacles and uncertainty. This perspective shift from fear to faith is essential for successful manifestation. By embracing this mindset, you open yourself up to new possibilities and opportunities that align with your goals.

The Science Behind Manifestation: Perspective Meets Reality

While manifestation might seem abstract, there's science behind it. The Law of Reversibility, derived from quantum physics, explains that if a feeling can produce a circumstance, then that circumstance can produce a feeling. This means that your perspective—how you think and feel—can directly shape your reality. Dr. Joe Dispenza, author and leading figure in neuroscience, explains that mental rehearsal changes the brain's wiring, making it easier to manifest the behaviors and outcomes you desire. This scientific perspective on manifestation reinforces the idea that our thoughts and emotions are powerful tools in creating our future.[3]

Mind is for manifesting ideas, not for holding them.

Dispenza's work highlights the importance of mental rehearsal in shaping our reality. By repeatedly visualizing a desired outcome, you can rewire your brain to support the behaviors and habits that lead to that outcome. This process involves creating detailed mental images of your goals, then mentally rehearsing the steps needed to achieve them. Over time, this practice strengthens the neural pathways associated with those behaviors, making it easier to act in ways that support your goals.

This understanding of the science behind manifestation also emphasizes the role of emotions in shaping our reality. Emotions are powerful drivers of behavior, and by cultivating positive emotions, you can create a more empowering and fulfilling reality. This requires consciously choosing to focus on thoughts and feelings that align with your goals, rather than allowing negative emotions to dictate your actions. By managing your emotional state, you can influence your behavior and, ultimately, your reality.

Overcoming Adversity: The Perspective of Resilience

Success isn't just about winning; it's also about how you handle losses. Every setback is a reminder that the other side of winning exists. Understanding this reality is crucial because it shifts your perspective from fearing failure to seeing it as a natural part of the journey. Neil deGrasse Tyson reminds us that simply being alive is a victory against incredible odds, and wasting our potential is a disservice to that victory.[4] This perspective on life encourages resilience, teaching us to push through adversity with the understanding that every loss is just another step toward success.

Resilience is a key component of success, and it's rooted in your perspective on failure. When you see failure as an opportunity to learn and grow, it becomes a building block rather than a stumbling block. This shift in perspective allows you to bounce back from setbacks with renewed determination and focus. It also helps you maintain a positive attitude in the face of challenges, which is essential for long-term success.

Resilience also involves adaptability. The ability to adjust your approach in response to changing circumstances is crucial for overcoming adversity. This requires a flexible mindset and a willingness to explore new strategies and solutions. By cultivating this adaptability, you can navigate challenges more effectively and turn obstacles into opportunities.

Mental Preparation: Surrendering the Uncontrollable

Preparing for setbacks, rather than expecting them, is a powerful mental approach to success. This mindset allows you to let go of what you can't control and focus entirely on what you can. By releasing the pressure tied to the fear of failure, you create the freedom to perform at your highest level. Additionally, setting clear and achievable goals fosters positive emotions by reinforcing the belief that progress is attainable. This combination of mental readiness and goal clarity helps sustain motivation and resilience, even when facing challenges.

Mental preparation is a critical aspect of success, and it's deeply connected to your perspective on control. By accepting that some things are beyond your control, you can focus your energy on what you can influence. This shift in perspective reduces anxiety and increases your ability to perform under pressure. It also helps you maintain a sense of balance and perspective, which is essential for long-term success.

The Importance of a Clear Vision: Setting the Course

Having a clear vision is essential for generating positive emotions and staying motivated. When your goals are clear, every step forward reinforces your progress. This process is deeply tied to your perspective, because how you see your journey influences your emotional response to it. By setting specific, achievable goals, you create a journey filled with moments of positive reinforcement, keeping you engaged and committed to your path. This clarity in vision is what drives successful individuals to maintain their focus and achieve their goals.

A clear vision acts as a compass, guiding your actions and decisions. It provides a sense of direction and purpose, helping you stay focused on your long-term goals. This clarity also makes it easier to prioritize your efforts and make decisions that align with your vision. When you know where you're headed, you can make choices that support your progress and avoid distractions that could lead you off course.

This clear vision also helps you maintain motivation during challenging times. When you encounter obstacles, your vision acts as a reminder of why you started and what you're working toward. This perspective shift from focusing on the challenge to focusing on the goal can help you stay motivated and resilient in the face of adversity. By keeping your vision at the forefront of your mind, you can navigate challenges with confidence and determination.

Mentors Can Help You Visualize Your Future

Mentorship is a powerful tool on the path to success. Learning from those who have already achieved their goals can transform your perspective and provide invaluable guidance as you navigate challenges. Mentors offer more than advice—they inspire a shift in mindset, helping you avoid common pitfalls and focus on long-term vision. Success is not just about hard work, but also about strategic thinking and cultivating the right mindset.

Over the years, as I've explored potential paths for my future, I've found immense value in the teachings of individuals on social media who share their expertise across various fields. I call them my "online mentors," as they've profoundly shaped my knowledge and perspectives. Entrepreneurs Patrick Bet-David and Cody Sanchez have offered insights on building and buying businesses. In real estate investing, figures like Robert Kiyosaki and Grant Cardone have expanded my understanding of wealth creation. For health and science, Andrew Huberman, Peter Attia, Lex Friedman, Gary Brecka, and Peter Diamandis have provided valuable insights on optimizing well-being. In psychology, mindset, and motivation, mentors like Jocko Willink, Jordan Peterson, Chris Williamson, Ed Mylett, Tony Robbins, Steven Bartlett, Jay Shetty, and Brian Tracy have shared philosophies that inspire resilience and personal growth.

Although I've yet to have a personal mentor at the age of twenty-one, these "online mentors" have played a significant role in helping me cultivate a well-rounded perspective and fueling my passion for continuous learning. Their collective wisdom has been a cornerstone in my journey of growth and development. Each of these individuals has helped me visualize not just the person I want to become but also the steps to get there.

Patrick Bet-David, in particular, personifies the qualities of a complete leader. As a polymath, he is a role model for aspiring polymaths like myself who enjoy the journey of developing a high knowledge-base in many different subjects. He not only educates and inspires, but also leads by example. Patrick's ability to articulate complex ideas, use powerful metaphors, and maintain emotional poise under pressure has influenced me greatly. His emphasis on emotional intelligence—the ability to stay composed and focused in challenging situations—is something I strive to emulate in both my personal and professional life.

Mentorship is not only about acquiring knowledge but also about advancing accountability. Mentors provide a level of support and encouragement that helps you stay on track. They hold you accountable for your actions, push you to maintain focus, and remind you of your goals when setbacks arise. This kind of support is essential for long-term success, as it cultivates resilience and a forward-thinking mindset.

The power of mentorship lies in its ability to help you visualize the future you want while equipping you with the tools to achieve it. Whether through direct interaction or by absorbing the wisdom of those who share their journeys online, mentorship offers a pathway to personal growth and self-discovery. It reminds us that no journey is taken alone and that the guidance of others can illuminate the road ahead, helping us reach our full potential.

Diverse Perspectives on Success

Inky Johnson's story is one of remarkable resilience and transformation. As a standout college football player at the University of Tennessee, he was on track for a career in the NFL—a dream he had nurtured since childhood. However, his life took an unexpected turn during a routine game in 2006. A single tackle caused a severe injury to his right arm and shoulder, leaving him permanently paralyzed on one side. This moment could have shattered him, but instead it became a turning point.

Faced with the reality that his lifelong dream of playing professional football was no longer possible, Johnson shifted his perspective. Rather than focusing on what he had lost, he chose to seek guidance from those who could help him redefine success and purpose. This led him to mentors who shared wisdom on perseverance, faith, and embracing life's challenges. These mentors didn't just teach him strategies for success; they showed him how to cultivate inner peace and find fulfillment beyond external achievements.

Through his guidance and his own introspection, Johnson learned to channel his passion and energy into motivational speaking. Today, he shares his story with audiences worldwide, inspiring them to focus on their

A mind is like a parachute.
It doesn't work if it is not open.

Frank Zappa

purpose and values. His story highlights how seeking guidance during adversity can open doors to new perspectives and opportunities. Johnson's ability to find purpose beyond his original dreams is a powerful reminder that even in the face of life's most challenging moments, we can redefine our paths and discover success that is aligned with our authentic selves.

The journey to success can be compared to finding different ways to arrive at a specific number—like the number 10. There are countless methods to reach it: 9+1, 8+2, 20/2, or even 1,000,000-999,990. Each equation represents a unique approach to achieving the same goal. Similarly, in life, "10" can symbolize happiness, financial freedom, good health, or personal fulfillment. The challenge arises when people assume that their way is the only correct way to reach these goals. This perspective can limit not only their potential but also their understanding of others' journeys. By embracing the idea that there are multiple paths to success, we open ourselves to the beauty of discovering our own unique route and appreciating the diverse approaches of those around us. Success, after all, is deeply personal, and its value lies in how it aligns with our individual aspirations and experiences.

Success isn't just about personal achievement; it's also about how we use our vision to uplift others and how we stay true to our own values and aspirations. Giang's analogy of infinite paths to success reinforces the idea that there's no one-size-fits-all approach. The key is finding the path that aligns with your values and aspirations, just as Johnson advises pursuing what truly captures your heart.

Inspiration provides the spark that ignites your passion and drives you toward your goals. It offers a fresh perspective on what's possible and encourages you to think bigger and dream more boldly. This inspiration can come from a variety of sources: books, podcasts, speeches, or conversations with others who have achieved success. By exposing yourself to diverse perspectives, you can gain new insights and ideas that can help you achieve your goals.

Inspiration also serves as a reminder of what's possible. When you see others achieving their goals, it reinforces your belief that you can do the same. This perspective shift from doubt to belief is crucial for success. By surrounding yourself with positive influences and role models, you can cultivate a mindset of possibility and create a more empowering reality. While the paths to success are many, the underlying principles of following your heart and defining your own journey are universal.

Throughout this chapter, we've explored the profound impact that visualization and perspective have on our lives. From using visualization as a GPS to understanding the science behind manifestation, the key takeaway is clear: how you see the world shapes your reality. By shifting your perspective from passive to active, from *want* to *will*, you unlock the power to turn your dreams into tangible outcomes. Now it's time to put these principles into practice. Start by visualizing your goals with clarity, expanding your thinking, and setting specific, actionable steps. Embrace discipline and routine, learn from mentors, and draw inspiration from those who have walked the path before you. Remember, success is not just about hard work; it's also about strategic thinking, continuous self-improvement, and the power of perspective. By embracing these concepts, you take the first step toward a future filled with success and fulfillment. The possibilities are endless, and the only limit is the one you set for yourself.

As you move forward, remember that your thoughts, words, and actions are interconnected. The perspective you hold today will shape the reality you experience tomorrow. Embrace the power of visualization and perspective, and watch as your life transforms in ways you never thought possible. The journey may be challenging, but with the right mindset, the rewards are boundless.

11
From Helplessness to Ownership
Choosing Accountability Over Victimhood

The way we perceive ourselves and the world around us fundamentally shapes our lives. The relationship you have with yourself sets the tone for the relationships you have with everyone else. Our internal dialogue, beliefs, and mindset act as the foundation upon which all other aspects of our lives are built. If we nurture a healthy, positive relationship with ourselves, we naturally attract and cultivate positive relationships with others. Conversely, if we allow negativity, self-doubt, and a victimhood mentality to take root, it impacts every interaction, decision, and outcome in our lives.

Often, we tend to blame others for negative outcomes because it feels easier and more emotionally satisfying than confronting uncomfortable realities. This inclination stems from a deeper psychological need to preserve our self-image. In a world where fairness is often idealized, the label "victim" becomes a powerful term, making us feel moral and justified in our suffering. However, this victimhood mentality breeds irresponsibility and negligence, allowing us to walk the conventional path of blame—where we vindicate ourselves of accountability and place the burden of our problems on others.

Defeating a victim mindset requires reconnecting with our inner compass, the steady guide that reminds us of our power to choose how we respond to life's challenges. When we're stuck in a victim mindset, we feel disconnected—adrift and controlled by external forces. This disconnect often drowns out the voice of our inner compass, making it harder to recognize our capacity to reclaim agency over our lives.

Understanding the connection between our mindset and our reality is the first step toward shifting from a mindset of lack and limitation to one of empowerment and possibility. Those who seek to be different, who strive to be rational and take responsibility for their actions, understand that true growth comes from walking the path less taken. This chapter will explore how our thoughts shape our reality, the importance of self-awareness, and the transformative power of embracing responsibility. By shifting from a victimhood mentality to one of personal accountability, we can break free from the constraints of blame and start building a life rooted in purpose and self-awareness.

The Roots of Victim Mentality

Victimhood mentality is not just a passing thought; it's an acquired personality trait and coping mechanism, often rooted in early life experiences. From a young age, many people are conditioned to believe that when things go wrong, it's easier and safer to blame others than to confront their own role in the situation. This mentality is further reinforced by societal norms that encourage a sense of entitlement, leading individuals to feel they deserve more than they currently have. When these expectations go unmet, dissatisfaction and unhappiness take hold, further entrenching the victimhood mentality.

However, victimhood doesn't always originate in childhood. It can develop later in life as a response to significant hardships or betrayals. Major life catastrophes such as financial ruin, job loss, or natural disasters can strip away a person's sense of agency, making it easier to adopt a "poor me" mindset. Chronic health issues or persistent pain can similarly create a sense of helplessness, reinforcing the belief that life is happening *to* them rather than *for* them. These experiences, while deeply challenging, can become the foundation for a mindset that views obstacles as insurmountable and life as inherently unfair.

Once entrenched, this mentality can be difficult to escape. The formula for measuring happiness ("Reality − Expectation = Happiness") illustrates how this mindset can become a trap. When our expectations are unrealistic, the gap between what we want and what we have widens, leading to frustration and a sense of injustice. Over time, this gap can develop feelings of bitterness and resentment, fueling a downward spiral of negativity. Additionally, victimhood often comes with a powerful inner narrative: "There's nothing I can do. I'm doomed." This self-defeating belief system perpetuates the cycle, making it increasingly difficult to break free. Victimhood can feel safe because it absolves the individual of responsibility and action. Yet, in reality, it creates a prison of stagnation and missed opportunities for growth.

To combat this mindset, it's essential to balance realistic expectations with the drive to improve. While lowering expectations may help close the gap between reality and desire, the ultimate goal is not to settle for less but to strengthen a mindset of empowerment and resilience. Life's challenges, no matter how difficult, can be reframed as opportunities for growth rather than insurmountable barriers. By understanding the roots of victim mentality—whether from early conditioning or life's later blows—we can begin to dismantle its hold and reclaim our sense of agency.

Consequences of Victimhood Mentality

Research by Dr. Rahav Gabray highlights that people who identify as victims tend to dwell on negative feelings for longer periods, making them less open to other perspectives and more likely to avoid accountability for the harm they may cause. This prolonged rumination not only instills a sense of helplessness but also stirs feelings of envy and resentment, further isolating the individual from positive social interactions.[1]

Jim Ferrell, an author and psychologist, adds that individuals often cling to the "innocence" they find in their suffering. This attachment to victimhood provides a perverse sense of moral superiority, allowing them to justify their inaction and blame others for their misfortunes. However, this mindset ultimately leads to a downward spiral of negative emotions and missed opportunities for growth. Instead of seeking solutions, individuals trapped in a victimhood mentality become fixated on their grievances, which hinders their ability to move forward and create a better life.[2]

The Cycle of Lack and Negativity

Victimhood mentality often thrives in a cycle of lack and negativity. Dr. Joe Dispenza, a prominent figure in neuroscience and spirituality, who I referred to in the last chapter, explains how focusing on what we don't have—be it finances, time, or energy—traps us in a vicious cycle. When we obsess over lack, our thoughts generate specific chemicals in the body that create a frequency reflecting that scarcity. This isn't just a fleeting moment of negativity; it has profound physiological effects.

These negative thoughts and the accompanying emotional states become stored in the body, particularly in what Dispenza refers to as the "second energy center". For example, when you feel guilty or unhappy, your brain produces chemicals that reinforce those feelings, creating a feedback loop of negativity. As you continue to dwell on these emotions, you generate more thoughts that align with them, producing more of the same chemicals. This cycle drains energy from the brain, storing it in the body, and conditions us to remain in a perpetual state of survival, with only 5 percent of our energy remaining in the brain and 95 percent trapped in the body.[3]

One of the most insidious habits people fall into is the constant focus on their problems—thinking about them, talking about them, and mentally rehearsing them. What many don't realize is that this habit actually feeds those problems, making them grow larger in your mind. The more energy we dedicate to our problems, the more they consume us. This phenomenon, known in psychology as *rumination*, is one of the key symptoms of depression. It refers to a repetitive, almost compulsive focus on pain, difficulties, or failures, which only serves to deepen the emotional distress. This perpetual state of rumination leaves us with little mental clarity or energy to make positive changes in our lives. Instead, we become conditioned to view the world through a lens of scarcity and limitation, reinforcing a victimhood mentality that is incredibly difficult to break free from.

Breaking the Cycle

Breaking the negativity cycle requires a conscious shift in focus—from lack to abundance, from negativity to possibility. It's about reclaiming the energy that has been drained by obsessive thoughts of what's missing in our lives and redirecting it toward creating the life we desire. This isn't just about thinking positively; it's about fundamentally altering the way we interact with our thoughts and emotions.

Dispenza emphasizes the importance of becoming aware of the thoughts driving your emotional state. By catching yourself in moments of negative thinking and deliberately choosing to focus on something positive, you begin to change the chemical responses in your body. Over time, this practice can help you shift out of survival mode and into a state of creation, where *you are no longer a victim of your circumstances but an active participant in shaping your reality.*[4] Imagine trying to explain all of your problems to someone whose struggles are far greater than yours. You might say, "I'm depressed because don't have a girlfriend. Money is tight. Life feels hard." But the person listening, who is facing life-threatening challenges every day, wouldn't hesitate to swap places with you in an instant. They'd sign on the dotted line, eager to trade their genuine hardships for your perceived difficulties.

This scenario underscores the power of perspective. What may feel overwhelming to you might seem insignificant to someone facing much more severe challenges. It reminds us that our problems are often relative, and we must be mindful of how we frame them. Shifting our perspective to focus on what we *do* have—health, opportunities, or even the simple freedom to make choices—can help us realize that our issues are manageable in the grand scheme of things. Life may feel hard at times, but when compared to real adversity, it becomes clear that practicing gratitude and adjusting our perspective can dramatically alter our outlook on life.

> *"If we all put our problems in a pile, I guarantee you would take yours and run."* —Kamaru Usman

The principles of the Law of Attraction reinforce this idea, emphasizing that where you direct your energy determines your outcomes. When you focus on complaints, your energy channels into lower frequencies, such as doubt, worry, and fear. Conversely, shifting your focus to envisioning possibilities raises your energy and opens the door to new opportunities. By asking "what if" questions—"What if all my needs were met?"—you engage in a mindset of potential and positivity. This shift in focus helps break free from a victimhood mentality, allowing you to embrace a world of opportunity and empowerment.

This shift in perspective is crucial for moving away from a victimhood mentality and stepping into a more empowered, fulfilling way of living. When life gets tough, and you feel like giving up, remind yourself that somewhere in the world, someone is lying on a hospital bed, desperately begging for a second chance at life. Recognize that you are blessed with health, good friends, and basic necessities like running water. There are no excuses not to push hard and live life with a smile. This mindset, rooted in gratitude, fuels resilience and helps you avoid falling into a victimhood mentality.

The concept that our thoughts significantly influence our happiness and well-being is a central tenet in positive psychology. It emphasizes that maintaining thoughts that are good, decent, and full of faith can lead to greater happiness and health, as it is ultimately our thoughts that decide whether we will be happy or unhappy, healthy or unhealthy. The happiest people, as this perspective suggests, are those who think the happiest, most interesting, and finest thoughts. This idea reinforces the principle that our mental focus shapes our reality, encouraging us to cultivate positive and uplifting thoughts to build a life of joy and fulfillment.

Consider the following everyday examples to illustrate the impact of shifting focus from lack to gratitude:

"I wish I had better shoes." *vs.* "At least I have shoes to wear."

"I am tired of working." *vs.* "I am grateful I have a job."

"This house is too small." *vs.* "I am thankful I have a roof over my head."

"I hate waking up early." *vs.* "I am glad I get to see another day."

"This shirt is old." *vs.* "I am grateful I have clothes to wear."

"I don't like this weather." *vs.* "I am glad I can feel the rain on my skin."

"I wish I had a better car." *vs.* "I am thankful I have a way to get around."

"I'm bored." *vs.* "I have the time to explore new things."

"I wish my phone was newer." *vs.* "I am lucky to have a phone."

"I don't like these leftovers." *vs.* "I am glad I have food to eat."

By changing your thoughts, you change your emotions, and by changing your emotions, you reclaim your energy and power. This mindset shift is essential for breaking the cycle of lack and negativity, paving the way for a life of empowerment and fulfillment.

The Importance of Introspection and Self-Awareness

In our fast-paced world, we often find ourselves caught up in a relentless cycle of doing, rarely taking the time to simply be. Deepak Chopra highlights a significant issue in modern life: our inability to sit quietly and reflect. He observes that we have become "human doings" rather than "human beings," constantly occupied with tasks, responsibilities, and distractions. This constant state of activity prevents us from connecting with our inner selves and understanding our true desires and purpose.

Chopra also suggests that taking time each day to be unoccupied and ask introspective questions like, "Who am I?", "What do I want?", and, "What is my purpose?" is crucial for personal growth. These moments of stillness allow us to step back from the chaos of daily life and gain clarity on what truly matters. Without this self-reflection, we may find ourselves merely reacting to life's circumstances rather than consciously shaping our path. Many people, Chopra notes, are unaware of their inner turmoil because they focus on external solutions, seeking immediate relief through superficial means like medication or distractions, without delving into the deeper causes of their distress. This lack of introspection keeps them trapped in a cycle of dissatisfaction, preventing them from realizing their full potential.[5]

The Impact of Our Upbringing

Our perception of life's challenges is often shaped by the environment we grew up in. If we were raised in a household where complaints, criticism, and a victimhood mentality were prevalent, we are more likely to view situations as adversities rather than opportunities. These early influences can deeply ingrain a mindset of scarcity and limitation, making it difficult to break free from negative thinking patterns. However, this mindset can be changed. By becoming aware of the impact our upbringing has had on our worldview, we can start to consciously shift our perspective. This process involves recognizing the automatic negative thoughts that arise in response to challenges and replacing them with more constructive and empowering thoughts. Changing this deeply ingrained mindset requires time and effort, but it is entirely possible. As we gradually replace old, limiting beliefs with new, empowering ones, we begin to see life's challenges not as insurmountable obstacles but as opportunities for growth and learning. This transformation from a victimhood mentality to one of empowerment is a key step in creating a life filled with purpose and fulfillment.

Transitioning from the broader theme of self-awareness, a practical metaphor can help us manage our emotions. Imagine emotional energy as a bucket of water. Some days, we wake up with an abundance of this emotional energy, which can feel overwhelming. If left unmanaged, this energy might be mistaken for negative emotions like anxiety or depression. The true superpower is not in suppressing emotions but in consciously choosing how to direct that energy—whether into anger, determination, or joy. *This perspective empowers us to take control of our emotional states rather than being at their mercy.* By consciously directing our emotional energy, we avoid falling into a victimhood mentality and instead shape our experiences through proactive choices.

> *"Don't allow yourself to be heard any longer griping about public life, not even with your own ears."* —*Marcus Aurelius*

Building on the theme of managing one's inner life, Marcus Aurelius, a Roman emperor and Stoic philosopher, offered wisdom on the dangers of complaining—even in solitude. He recognized that the act of complaining fosters a mindset of helplessness and weakness. According to Aurelius, *power is as much about perception as it is about reality.*[6] By refraining from complaints, we project an image of strength and self-sufficiency, which in turn strengthens our self-perception. This Stoic rule is a lesson in mental resilience, encouraging us to channel our energy into action rather than dwelling on negativity. By refusing to complain and focusing on overcoming obstacles, we avoid the trap of victimhood and cultivate a mindset geared toward empowerment and success.

Similarly, author Jay Shetty explores how shifting from blame to accountability can transform our approach to conflict and personal growth. He discusses how society often teaches us to blame others when we experience conflict or disagreement. When we share our frustrations with friends, they tend to reinforce our perception that the other person is at fault. However, Shetty suggests that the most empowering question we can ask ourselves in these moments is: "What is my accountability in this situation?" Instead of placing blame externally or internally, he encourages us to explore our role in the conflict. By embracing this perspective, we shift from a victimhood mentality to one of personal growth and self-awareness, recognizing that we have a part in every situation we encounter.[7]

This idea of accountability connects seamlessly to the way we value ourselves and others. Chris Williamson, host of *Modern Wisdom* podcast, challenges us to consider how we value ourselves and others, emphasizing the importance of genuine self-love. He explores the uncomfortable question of whether people love us for who we are or for what we do. He notes that being loved for who we are feels more genuine and enduring, while being loved for what we do feels transactional and temporary. Williamson then turns the question inward, asking whether we love ourselves for who we are or for what we do. He points out the hypocrisy in our desire for unconditional love from others while our self-love is often contingent on our achievements. This reflection encourages us to align our self-love with the kind of love we seek from the world, helping us avoid the pitfalls of a victimhood mentality where our self-worth is tied solely to external accomplishments.[8]

Empathy and Active Listening as Tools for Alleviating Suffering

One of the most profound ways to connect with others and alleviate their suffering is through empathy and active listening. When we fully accept someone and listen to them without judgment or the need to offer advice, we create a space of healing and connection. Neuroscience supports this, showing that the amygdala—the brain's emotional center—can be calmed simply by being heard with deep empathy.

There are four key elements in supporting others: acceptance, affection, appreciation, and attention. These elements create an environment where people feel truly seen and understood, significantly reducing their emotional distress. Instead of trying to fix their problems or offer solutions, simply being present and empathetic can have a transformative effect on their emotional state. This approach strengthens our own relationships by nurturing deeper connections, helping us build resilience against the victimhood mindset.

The relationships we cultivate with others are a direct reflection of the relationship we have with ourselves. If we want to improve our relationships, we must start by working on ourselves. This means developing self-awareness, practicing self-love, and ensuring that we are emotionally healthy and whole.

The Impact of Positive Relationships

When we approach relationships from a place of self-awareness and empathy, we naturally attract and nurture positive connections. These relationships, in turn, reinforce our sense of self-worth and empower us to face life's challenges with greater resilience. On the other hand, if we neglect our own emotional health and remain trapped in negative thought patterns, our relationships will likely reflect that negativity, leading to conflict and dissatisfaction.

By focusing on self-improvement and cultivating positive relationships, we create a support network that helps us maintain a healthy perspective. This network can be a powerful source of strength, helping us avoid the pitfalls of a victimhood mentality and encouraging us to continue growing and evolving in all aspects of our lives. As we consider the benefits of positive relationships and self-awareness, it's important to acknowledge the detrimental effects when these elements are missing. The consequences of embracing a victimhood mentality are far-reaching and often destructive. When we adopts this mindset, we become more prone to negative emotions, self-absorption, and a reluctance to take responsibility for our actions.

Moving from Excuses to Accountability

Excuses often serve as the barriers we place between ourselves and our potential. They are the justifications we use to avoid taking action, facing challenges, or accepting responsibility. While excuses might provide temporary comfort, they ultimately keep us stuck in a cycle of inaction and mediocrity. Excuses cannot build relationships, success, or wealth; they cannot forge character, discipline, or resilience. In essence, excuses are the inverse of growth and progress.

> *Responsibility is accepting that you are the cause and the solution of the matter.*

Here are some examples that highlight the limitations of excuses:

- Excuses can't build empires.
- Excuses can't build trust.
- Excuses can't build success.
- Excuses can't build strength.
- Excuses can't build character.
- Excuses can't build discipline.
- Excuses can't build courage.
- Excuses can't build resilience.
- Excuses can't build happiness.
- Excuses can't build confidence.

The common thread in all these statements is that excuses prevent growth. Whether it's building an empire or simply building trust in a relationship, excuses only serve to delay or derail our progress. They surrender our power to external circumstances, reinforcing a victimhood mentality that keeps us from realizing our full potential.

To move beyond the limitations of excuses, we must embrace accountability. Alex Hormozi succinctly explains this concept: "Power follows the blame finger."[9] Wherever we point the blame, we also transfer our power. If we blame the government, our partner, or our circumstances for our lack of success, we give them control over our lives. Conversely, when we take full responsibility—saying, "It's my fault"—we reclaim that power.

Hormozi's perspective is especially powerful because it applies even in situations where the circumstances may not be entirely our fault. Whether it's losing a leg at birth or facing other significant challenges, the choice remains: Do we give up and accept the limitations, or do we find a way to overcome them? By choosing to overcome, we take control of our narrative and our future. This shift from blame to accountability is crucial in breaking free from a victimhood mentality. It's not about self-blame or guilt; it's about recognizing that, regardless of the hand we've been dealt, we have the power to shape our response. This mindset of ownership and responsibility enables us to build success, trust, strength, and all the other things that excuses cannot.

Former college athlete Zack Tyree, in his speech at Boise State University's graduation ceremony, provided a poignant reminder of the power of choice. He compared words like "enemies" and "friends," "lying" and "truth," "failure" and "success," emphasizing that these words have the same number of letters. The implication is that life presents us with choices, and it is up to us to choose the better side. Tyree's message reinforces the idea that we have the autonomy to define our path by opting for positivity, truth, and success, thereby overcoming a victimhood mentality.[10]

In a powerful scene from *Rocky VI*, Rocky Balboa delivers a tough-love speech to his son about resilience. The essence of the message is clear: Life is tough and will knock you down, but true success comes from getting back up and continuing to move forward.[11] It's a reminder that life isn't about how hard you can hit, but how hard you can get hit and keep going. The scene emphasizes that there's no time for playing the victim, highlighting the importance of resilience and determination in overcoming adversity. It's a call to embrace a mindset of strength and perseverance, no matter the challenges faced.

Comedian Jimmy Carr offers a blunt reflection on mood and behavior. He argues that if you're in a bad mood all the time, it's not just about being in a bad mood—it's indicative of a deeper issue, possibly poor treatment of yourself or others. He emphasizes that your mood is revealed in how you treat people in everyday situations, like how you interact with a waitress or react to a speeding ticket. Carr suggests that life will inevitably throw challenges your way, but your reactions to these small moments reveal a lot about your overall mindset. This perspective encourages us to take responsibility for our moods and actions, recognizing that how we respond to life's minor inconveniences can either reinforce a victimhood mentality or help us build resilience.[12]

When life feels stagnant, the first step toward transformation is recognizing the need for change. It starts with getting fed up—tired of the same routines, the same results, and the same actions that lead nowhere. Change doesn't happen on its own; it requires effort, intention, and the willingness to step out of your comfort zone. This mindset challenges complacency and encourages us to take ownership of our lives. By embracing the discomfort of dissatisfaction, we can find the motivation to pursue something better, rejecting a passive approach and actively working toward growth and progress.

Eric Thomas, motivational speaker, author, and pastor, shares a pivotal moment of self-realization. One day, he woke up and decided to stop making excuses and playing the blame game. He looked at himself in the mirror and asked, "What are you doing? Wake up! It's showtime! Let's go!" This moment marked a turning point where he took full responsibility for his life and actions, deciding to move forward with purpose and determination.[13] Thomas's message is one of empowerment, urging us to stop feeling sorry for ourselves and to take action. This perspective shifts the focus from external excuses to internal accountability, rejecting a victimhood mentality and embracing a mindset of self-empowerment.

Tyrese Gibson, in *How to Get Out of Your Own Way*, offers advice about overcoming excuses and self-pity. He points out that excuses sound best to the person making them and urges people to stop feeling sorry for themselves. Instead, he calls for awakening the "beast inside" and taking advantage of the resources and opportunities available. Gibson emphasizes that if you have a problem with your life or environment, you need to do something about it. His message is one of self-empowerment: if you want something, go get it. This perspective encourages taking responsibility for your own success and rejecting the notion of being a victim of your circumstances.[14]

It's not our circumstances that shape us, but how we respond to them. Drawing on the wisdom of the Greek philosopher Epictetus, success and failure are determined by what we do with what we have. This perspective encourages us to view challenges as opportunities for growth, rather than obstacles to our success. By adopting this mindset, we can avoid the trap of victimhood and cultivate resilience and a proactive approach to life.

Jay Shetty offers another key strategy for overcoming victimhood mentality by focusing on self-validation. He argues that whatever we seek from others—whether it's compliments, validation, or recognition— we should first give to ourselves. External validation will never truly satisfy us if we haven't learned to value ourselves internally. By building a foundation of self-worth that isn't dependent on the opinions of others, we free ourselves from the cycle of seeking external approval.[15] This empowers us to create a sense of fulfillment from within, helping us avoid the trap of a victimhood mentality.

Self-belief and resilience are essential when navigating life's challenges. While it's natural to feel down at times, the key is not to stay there. Eventually, we face a choice: give up or get back up and live fully. By shifting our focus from doubt to belief—not just in others, but in ourselves—we can build the strength to overcome obstacles and live with purpose and joy.

Let's use the metaphor of an orange to illustrate a profound truth about our, inner state. When you squeeze an orange, only orange juice comes out because that's what's inside. Similarly, when life squeezes us—through challenges or hurtful words—what comes out is a reflection of what's inside us. This perspective encourages us to take responsibility for our emotional responses. If we don't like what comes out, we have the power to change it. This mindset empowers us to reject blame and victimhood, embracing personal growth and self-improvement.

Author and business advisor Price Pritchett poses a thought-provoking question: "Which is more important—more positive thinking or less negative thinking?" Studies show that reducing negative thinking is more impactful. While positive thinking is important, cutting down on negative thoughts is where real progress is made. Pritchett identifies the "villain voice" in our heads—the critic, the demotivator, the doubter—and urges us to shut it down.[16] By focusing on reducing negative thinking, we eliminate barriers that hold us back, making way for a more empowered and positive mindset. This approach helps us avoid the trap of victimhood by learning to silence the inner critic and focus on what truly matters.

Denis Waitley, psychologist and author, contrasts losers and winners, highlighting that the difference lies in mindset and perception. Losers let things happen to them, seeing only challenges like thunderstorms or icy streets; while winners make things happen, spotting rainbows and putting on their ice skates. Losers take chances, hoping for the best, but winners make deliberate choices, shaping their outcomes. Waitley reminds us that we become what we think about most of the time.[17] By mastering their mindset, winners turn potential failure into victory. This perspective underlines the importance of choosing a winning mindset over victimhood, recognizing that control over our thoughts leads to control over our destiny.

Changing our mindset from one of lack to one of abundance, from excuses to accountability, requires constant self-reflection, a willingness to challenge deeply ingrained beliefs, and the courage to take responsibility for our actions and outcomes. However, the rewards of making this shift are immense. By choosing empowerment over victimhood, we open ourselves to a life filled with purpose, fulfillment, and success.

The journey from victimhood to empowerment is ongoing. Each day, we have the opportunity to choose how we respond to life's challenges, how we treat ourselves and others, and how we pursue our goals. By consistently choosing empowerment, we build the life we desire and deserve. As we move away from a victimhood mentality, it's also essential to recognize the importance of not rescuing others to the point where it enables their victimhood. As author and entrepreneur Donald Miller discusses in his book *Scary Close*, when we repeatedly rescue someone from their problems without allowing them to face the consequences, we drain our own energy and prevent them from learning valuable life lessons.[18] It's a difficult balance, especially for those with a compassionate nature, but sometimes we must let others struggle so they can develop the resilience needed to thrive.

Ultimately, victimhood mentality is not only unattractive but also counterproductive. It prevents individuals from reaching their full potential and creates a cycle of dependency and helplessness. Instead, those who take responsibility for their lives—who choose to overcome challenges rather than be defined by them—become true heroes. These are the people who inspire others and lead by example, showing that it's possible to rise above adversity and achieve greatness.

12
The Victory in Losing
Turning Failures into Foundations

Setbacks and failures are inevitable companions. However, it's not the failures themselves that define us, but rather how we respond to them. The art of turning losses into lessons is a transformative process that requires introspection, resilience, and a growth mindset. Through the wisdom of various individuals like Kobe Bryant, Michael Jordan, Trevor Moawad, Dewayne Noel, and David Goggins, we will explore the profound insights into navigating adversity and transforming setbacks into launchpads toward success. Each perspective offers unique approaches to facing challenges, embracing failure, and emerging stronger, wiser, and more resilient.

Failure, when viewed through the lens of our inner compass, becomes less about defeat and more about redirection. Our inner compass is not a guarantee of smooth sailing, but a guide that helps us navigate even the rough waters of setbacks. When we fail, it's an opportunity to pause, recalibrate, and listen more closely to what our inner compass is trying to tell us.

The Lorax by Dr. Seuss has a simply brilliant line: "Which way does the tree fall . . . ? A tree falls the way it leans. Be careful which way you lean."[1] The metaphor of the falling tree serves as a reminder to be mindful of our direction and choices. Just as a tree falls in the direction it leans, our actions and decisions dictate the outcomes we experience. By being aware of our inclinations and tendencies, we can better navigate toward success or failure. It underscores the importance of understanding the consequences of our actions and making intentional choices.

Our actions, perceptions, and decisions play a significant role in shaping the outcome of our endeavors. How we perceive situations, the actions we take, and the decisions we make all contribute to whether we succeed or fail. By recognizing the influence of these factors, we can proactively work towards achieving our goals. This highlights the importance of self-awareness and strategic decision-making in navigating through life's challenges and opportunities.

Reflecting on Failure

Reflection and analysis following failure are crucial for personal and professional growth. By examining why things didn't work out or why a failure occurred, we can gain valuable perception into our actions, decisions,

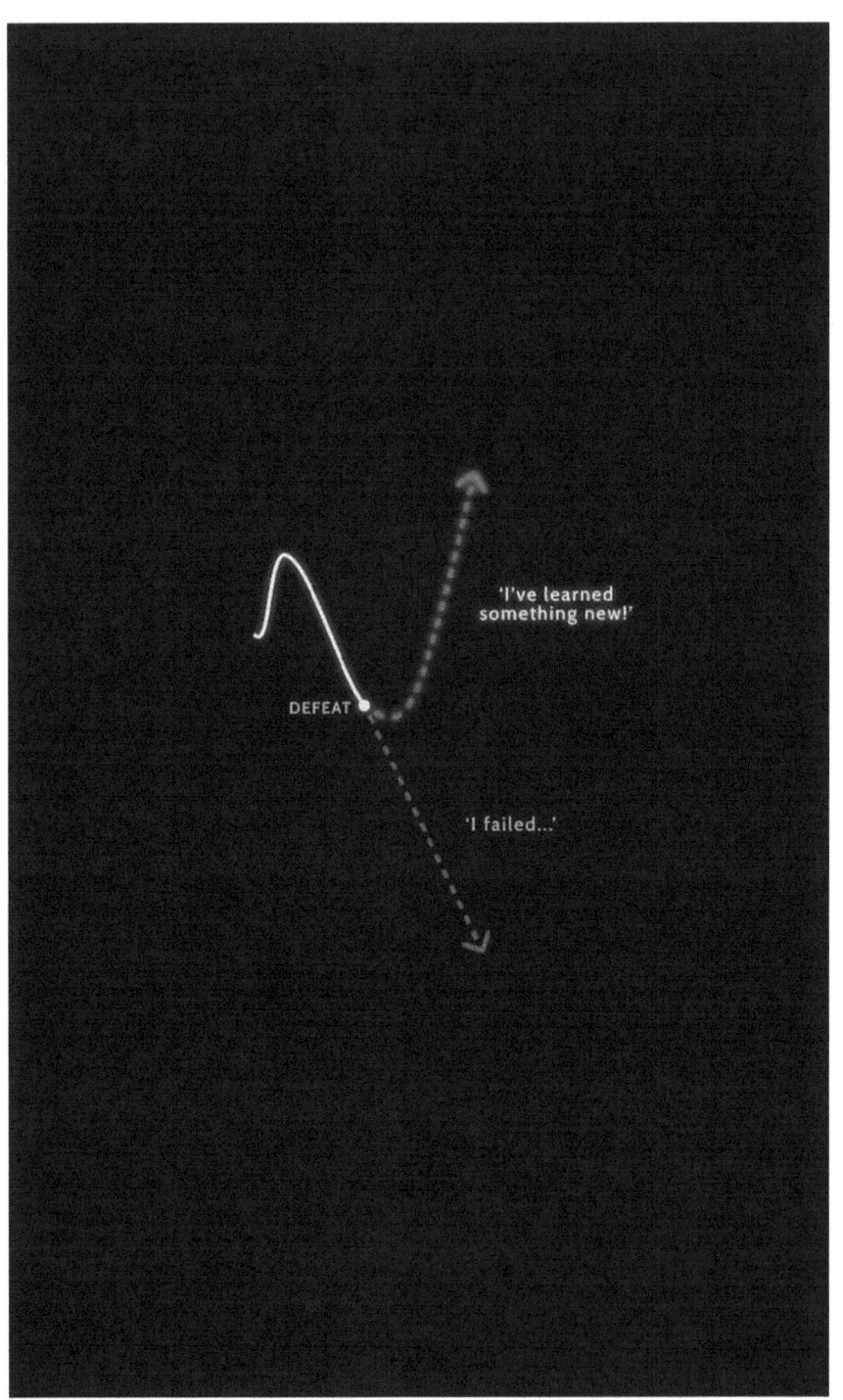

and circumstances. This process allows for a deeper understanding of what went wrong and how similar mistakes can be avoided in the future. It highlights the importance of introspection as a means of learning from setbacks and improving oneself.

Losing is winning if you learn from it.

Neglecting to learn from past mistakes can have significant consequences. Without reflection and analysis, we risk repeating the same errors, leading to continued failure and stagnation. Failing to recognize and address the root causes of failure perpetuates a cycle of setbacks and missed opportunities. It underscores the need to actively engage in self-assessment to break free from patterns of failure and pursue growth. Self-assessment is vital for personal and professional development. By critically evaluating our actions, decisions, and outcomes, we can identify areas for improvement and refine our strategies for success. Embracing self-assessment strengthens a mindset of continuous learning and adaptation, enabling us to navigate challenges more effectively. It emphasizes the proactive role we all play in our own growth journeys, highlighting the importance of accountability and self-awareness.

Embracing Doubt and Uncertainty

Kobe Bryant once said, "Doubt is a strange thing. There will be times when you succeed and times when you fail. Wasting your time doubting whether you are going successful or not it's pointless. You put one foot in front of the other, you control what you can control, and see what the outcome is."[2] We understand that doubt is a natural aspect of the journey toward success. Doubt may arise when we face failure or unexpected challenges in our endeavors, but we must recognize that doubt can be a hindrance, causing us to second-guess ourselves and our abilities.

However, Kobe understands that dwelling on doubt or surrendering to negativity only prolongs the process of learning from losses. Instead, he emphasizes the importance of confronting doubt head-on and using it as a catalyst for growth. Losses serve as valuable opportunities for learning and improvement. Shift your focus from dwelling on losses to concentrating on what you can control. Controlling the controllables. Rather than fixating on past failures, individuals should channel their energy into actionable steps for improvement.

> *"The windshield is bigger than the rearview mirror for a reason."* —Jelly Roll

Respect the past, learn from it, but don't get caught looking too long because without looking forward a crash is inevitable. We must use our new knowledge on the decision we make in the future. By prioritizing actions over doubts, you can maintain momentum and progress toward our goals. Despite experiencing losses, Kobe believes that consistent effort and dedication are key to overcoming uncertainty and achieving success. When a reporter once asked him, "How much harder will you work in this off-season to get back to the championship?" Kobe responded with determination: "I will push myself to exhaustion."[3] This response underscores his relentless drive to overcome challenges and improve. Setbacks should not deter us from our goals but rather motivate us to work harder and smarter.

Like Kobe, we can view losses as opportunities for self-analysis and growth. By embracing doubt as a temporary obstacle, reflecting on what went wrong, and identifying areas for improvement, we are able to extract valuable lessons from their setbacks. Kobe's own career serves as a testament to the power of resilience. He encountered numerous setbacks and challenges including injury, teammate friction, and playoff losses throughout his basketball career, but he remained committed to his craft and ultimately achieved greatness.

Learning from Setbacks

Michael Jordan once said, "I hate losing, but I only have to respect losing because losing is a part of winning. You never just win, you have to lose to win. How can I do things differently? How can I change? You have to look at yourself in the mirror because that's how things get started, and you have to be willing to change."[4] The first sentence highlights his fierce competitiveness and desire for success with his strong distaste for failure. He pairs this with a deep understanding of losing's role in the path to success and acknowledges the inevitability of failure in the pursuit of victory.

By expressing his dislike for losing while simultaneously acknowledging its importance, Jordan highlights the complexity of his relationship with failure. He recognizes that while losing may be painful, it also provides valuable lessons and opportunities for growth. This attitude demonstrates Jordan's resilience and determination to learn from setbacks, ultimately using them as fuel for future success. He respects the lessons learned from defeat while maintaining a relentless pursuit of victory. He understands that failure is not a sign of weakness but rather a necessary component of the journey towards greatness.

Jordan's mindset of "How can I do things differently? How can I change?" underscores the importance of self-reflection and adaptation in response to failure. He emphasizes the need to critically assess one's performance and approach, seeking ways to improve and evolve. This mindset reflects Jordan's proactive approach to failure, where he understands that true growth and progress require a willingness to adapt and evolve in the face of adversity. His perspective on failure encourages people to embrace setbacks as opportunities for growth and development. He challenges the notion that failure should be feared or avoided, instead advocating for a mindset that sees failure as a natural part of the journey toward success. He urges us to confront our shortcomings honestly and use them as fuel for improvement.

We know you have the talent and the skillset to succeed, but do you have the guts to fail?

Finding Strength in Adversity

On the *Impact Theory* podcast with Tom Bilyeu, author and sports psychologist Trevor Moawad tells a story that demonstrates the transformative power of turning losses into lessons. It is a story of an individual who faced academic struggles in high school but made a promise to his mother to take the SAT. Despite expecting to fail, he unexpectedly scored a remarkable 1480 out of 1600. When accused of cheating, he revealed he had tried but couldn't due to the test format. Recognizing his intelligence and this success, it motivated him to change his approach where he committed to attending classes, graduated, and went to community college. He went on to become a successful magazine entrepreneur. However, twelve years later, he discovered an error in his SAT score; his actual score was a 740. Despite this revelation, he acknowledged that his life had changed when he started believing in himself like a 1480.[5]

Moawad's story underscores the transformative power of perception and mindset. Despite his initial academic struggles, he perceived himself as intelligent and capable, which allowed him to maintain his belief in potential success. The revelation of his high score, whether accurate or not, served as a catalyst for him to embrace this perception of himself as smart and capable. This newfound confidence and self-perception likely influenced his following actions and decisions, leading to his success as a magazine entrepreneur. Adopting a positive perception of oneself and aligning actions with desired goals can facilitate the transformation of setbacks into opportunities for growth and success.

Embracing the Journey

Dewayne Noel, podcaster, YouTuber, and educator, once said, "The man who never fell has no glory. The man who fell and got back up, that's where his glory is. The man who fell twenty times and got up twenty-one times, that man has even greater glory. That man has more courage, way more courage, than the guy who was so strong from birth that he never fell, there's no glory in that."[6] This statement highlights the valor and honor in persistence and resilience. True glory is not found in never falling but in the act of getting back up after each fall. It is a concept that is well-known but more complicated to execute for the fact of learning from each fall.

By praising those who have fallen multiple times and still found the courage to rise again, Noel underscores the importance of perseverance and determination in achieving greatness. This perspective shifts the focus from flawless success to the journey of seeking out imperfections and areas of weakness, along with overcoming obstacles and setbacks.

This suggests that the true measure of glory lies in one's ability to persist in the face of adversity.

Noel highlights the strength found in persisting through failures, emphasizing that true courage lies in learning from adversity and growing stronger with each setback. He encourages us to reframe failure not as a mark of inadequacy, but as a testament to resilience and an essential step toward success. By praising the bravery of those who rise after falling, Noel inspires a mindset of optimism and determination, urging us to face challenges head-on and recognize each setback as an opportunity for growth and self-improvement.

Navigating Challenges with Perspective

Adversity is an inevitable part of life, presenting challenges that test both character and resolve. Success often depends not on the absence of obstacles but on how one processes and responds to them. The right perspective can transform setbacks into opportunities for growth, reminding us that failures don't have to define our journey. Instead, each difficult moment offers an opportunity to learn, adapt, and improve. Life's challenges, while daunting, serve as powerful tests of resilience and determination, shaping us into stronger individuals and reminding us that one difficult chapter doesn't dictate the entire story.

Developing Unstoppable Resilience

True resilience comes from an inner resolve to keep moving forward, no matter how difficult the circumstances become. It's about standing firm when life feels overwhelming and choosing to persevere through challenges rather than giving up. This mindset is built on the belief that setbacks are not the end but stepping stones to something greater. Even in the darkest moments, reminding yourself, "I'll keep going no matter what," fosters the kind of mental strength needed to navigate life's toughest trials. This unwavering determination transforms hardships into powerful lessons that fuel growth and success.

David Goggins, retired United States Navy SEAL, ultramarathon runner, author, and public speaker, is known for his perspective on over-

Life is like a ride.

Keep moving to keep balance.

coming mental barriers by focusing on the power of self-talk and mental toughness. His book *You Can't Hurt Me* is a powerful reminder that no matter what is being sent our way in life, we must say to ourselves on a daily basis, "You can't hurt me," and before you know it, it will become the truth. Not because you say it, but you have to put the work in to develop and callous the mind to believe that it's true.[7] Goggins encourages us to cultivate a mindset where we believe we are capable of overcoming any obstacle. He is consistent on the importance of disciplined efforts and developing a resilient mindset, even in the face of failure or adversity.

Practical strategies for cultivating resilience and maintaining momentum amidst challenges are essential to the process of turning losses into lessons. Setting achievable goals, maintaining a positive outlook, and embracing discomfort as a catalyst for growth are all strategies that not only can help us navigate adversity effectively, but also develop the mental toughness that is necessary to navigate hardship and achieve our goals. By adopting these practices, we are able to develop the persistence needed to overcome setbacks and extract valuable insights from each of our personal experiences. This enables each of us to transform losses into valuable lessons that contribute to our personal and professional development.

In life, the threads of failure are woven alongside those of success, each contributing to the richness of our experiences. The journey of turning losses into lessons is not simply about bouncing back from adversity, but about harnessing the transformative power of setbacks to propel ourselves forward. By embracing failure as a natural part of growth, adopting a resilient mindset, and learning from the wisdom of those who have walked the path before us, we empower ourselves to navigate life's challenges with courage, determination, and grace. It's through these diverse perspectives that we reshape our understanding of failure, seeing it not as a roadblock but as a guiding light toward personal and professional development. Ultimately, it's not the falls we take that define us, but the lessons we gather from them that shape our perspective and journey towards success.

Choose Your Hard

Navigating life's challenges not only tests our resilience but also induces significant changes in our brain's structure and function—a phenomenon known as neuroplasticity. This adaptive capacity enables the brain to reorganize itself in response to experiences, including adversity. Recent research has illuminated how exposure to adversity can lead to both adaptive and maladaptive neural changes. A study published in *Nature Neuroscience* examined individuals over time and found that early-life adversities could result in persistent alterations in brain morphology, particularly in regions associated with emotion regulation and cognitive processing. These structural changes were linked to increased anxiety levels in later life, underscoring the long-term impact of early stressors on mental health.[8]

However, the brain's plasticity also offers a pathway to recovery and growth. Engaging in positive experiences and therapeutic interventions can promote beneficial neural rewiring. For instance, cognitive-behavioral therapy (CBT) has been shown to facilitate neuroplastic changes that alleviate symptoms of depression and anxiety. By actively working to reshape thought patterns, individuals can ignite new, healthier neural connections, effectively countering the adverse effects of past experiences.[9]

Moreover, physical activities like aerobic exercise have been demonstrated to stimulate neurogenesis—the birth of new neurons—in the hippocampus, a brain region integral to memory and learning. This process not only enhances cognitive function but also contributes to emotional resilience, providing a biological foundation for improved mental health.[10] Understanding the brain's capacity for neuroplasticity highlights the importance of proactive strategies in overcoming adversity. By engaging in therapeutic practices, maintaining physical activity, and cultivating positive experiences, individuals can harness the brain's inherent adaptability to uphold resilience and well-being.

Life will always present difficulties, but we have the power to choose how we handle them. Whether it's communication, fitness, or financial habits, each has its own challenges.

- Being in debt is hard. Being financially disciplined is hard. Choose your hard.
- Obesity is hard. Being fit is hard. Choose your hard.
- Communication is hard. Not communicating is hard. Choose your hard.
- Marriage is hard. Divorce is hard. Choose your hard.

Life will never be easy, but you can choose your hard. Choose wisely.

Life is full of decisions, challenges, and setbacks, each of which offers an opportunity for growth and transformation. The ability to turn losses into lessons is a powerful testament to the importance of perspective. By reflecting on our experiences, setting intentional goals, and learning from our mistakes, we can shift our mindset from focusing on failures to embracing the opportunities they provide. This process empowers us to move forward with clarity, resilience, and purpose, using every experience as a catalyst to greater understanding and achievement.

1. Reflect on Your Values

- Action: Take time to reflect on your core values and priorities.
- Purpose: This ensures that your decisions align with what truly matters to you.

2. Define Your Goals

- S - Specific: Clearly define what you want to achieve with as much detail as possible.
- M - Measurable: Set criteria for measuring progress and success.
- A - Achievable: Ensure the goal is attainable with the resources and time you have.
- R - Relevant: Choose goals that align with your broader objectives and values.
- T - Time-bound: Assign a specific deadline for completion to create urgency and focus.

3. Assess the Pros and Cons

- Action: Carefully weigh the pros and cons of each option when faced with a decision.
- Purpose: This helps determine which path aligns best with your values and goals.

4. Cultivate Resilience

- Action: Develop mental and emotional resilience by practicing mindfulness, meditation, or stress-management techniques.
- Purpose: Resilience equips you to handle setbacks with strength and recover quickly, maintaining focus on long-term goals.

5. Consider the Long-Term Impact

- Action: Look beyond immediate gratification and consider the long-term consequences of your choices.
- Purpose: A long-term perspective helps avoid choices that feel good in the moment but are detrimental in the long run.

6. Accept What You Cannot Control

- Action: Focus on what you can influence and let go of what's beyond your control.
- Purpose: Accepting the uncontrollable allows you to channel your energy productively, reducing unnecessary stress and frustration.

7. Take Responsibility

- Action: Accept ownership of your decisions and their outcomes.
- Purpose: Owning your choices empowers you to take control of your life's direction.

8. Learn from Mistakes

- Action: Embrace failures and setbacks as opportunities for growth and learning.
- Purpose: Each mistake builds a foundation of better understanding and improvement.

9. Identify Patterns

- Action: Look for recurring themes or mistakes in your experiences to understand underlying causes.
- Purpose: Recognizing patterns helps you proactively address weaknesses and avoid repeating the same errors.

10. Seek Feedback from Others

- Action: Invite trusted mentors, friends, or colleagues to provide constructive feedback.
- Purpose: An external perspective can reveal blind spots, offering valuable insights for growth.

11. Adapt and Adjust

- Action: Be willing to adjust your course if necessary to stay aligned with your goals and values.
- Purpose: Flexibility is key to navigating life's unpredictability and staying on track.

12. Visualize the Bigger Picture

- Action: Regularly remind yourself of your ultimate goals and how your current decisions fit into that vision.
- Purpose: Visualizing the bigger picture ensures that momentary setbacks don't overshadow your long-term aspirations.

13. Take Incremental Action

- Action: Break large goals or challenges into smaller, manageable steps.
- Purpose: Small, consistent actions make progress feel attainable and reduce overwhelm when addressing setbacks.

14. Practice Gratitude

- Action: Reflect daily on what you're grateful for, including lessons learned from challenges.
- Purpose: Gratitude shifts your focus to the positive, fostering an optimistic mindset even during difficult times.

15. Celebrate Successes

- Action: Celebrate your victories, no matter how small.
- Purpose: Recognizing achievements fosters motivation and appreciation for the journey.

Adopting the mindset of turning losses into lessons is a lifelong journey that demands reflection, adaptability, and responsibility. By following these steps—reflecting on values, defining goals, and celebrating even small successes—you create a framework for growth and transformation. The power of perspective allows you to see setbacks not as barriers but as building blocks, turning each challenge into an opportunity for self-improvement. In the end, it's not the losses themselves that define us, but how we choose to learn from them and use them to shape a life of purpose and fulfillment.

13
Act NOW
The Courage to Begin

Taking action is the foundation upon which all success is built. Without it, even the most brilliant ideas and grand visions remain mere dreams, unfulfilled and unrealized. The importance of action cannot be overstated; it is the catalyst that transforms potential into reality. However, taking action often requires patience and perseverance, qualities that are not always easy to maintain in a world that increasingly values instant gratification. A powerful metaphor that encapsulates the importance of patience and perseverance in the pursuit of our goals is the story of the Chinese bamboo tree. This story vividly illustrates that the most significant and transformative growth often happens beneath the surface, invisible to the outside world, until the time is right for it to emerge.

The courage to act, even if only a small step, often comes from trusting our inner compass, even when the path ahead feels uncertain or intimidating. Our inner compass quietly points us toward what feels authentic and aligned with our values, but following its guidance requires bravery. It means stepping into the unknown, risking failure, and sometimes going against the expectations of others.

> "You don't have to be great to start, but you have to start to be great." —Zig Ziglar

The Chinese Bamboo Tree:
A Story of Patience and Persistence

This story perfectly captures the essence of patience, persistence, and the often unseen efforts required to achieve greatness. The growth process of the Chinese bamboo tree is nothing short of extraordinary. For the first five years of its life, the bamboo shows no visible signs of growth above the ground. During this time, it is slowly and methodically developing a complex and robust root system that will support its rapid growth later on. Day after day, the caretakers must water and fertilize the ground, trusting that their efforts are not in vain, even though there is no visible progress to reassure them.

It isn't until the fifth year that the bamboo finally breaks through the ground. And when it does, something incredible happens: Within just five weeks, the bamboo tree grows an astonishing ninety feet tall. This sudden and dramatic growth prompts an important question: Did the bamboo grow ninety feet in five weeks, or did it grow over five years? The answer is clear: It grew over five years. The years spent nurturing and developing its roots were just as crucial as the final, visible spurt of growth. Had the caretakers stopped watering and nurturing the bamboo at any point during those five years, the tree would have died underground, never having the chance to reach its full potential.

Now, imagine being the farmer who diligently waters the same spot in the dirt for five long years, with nothing to show for his work. The people in his village must have thought he was crazy, ridiculing him for his apparent lack of progress. They may have laughed at him, doubted his efforts, and questioned his sanity. Yet the farmer persisted, driven by the belief that his efforts would eventually pay off. When the bamboo finally shot out of the ground, the same people who once mocked him were left in awe, exclaiming, "Wow, look how fast it grew! I knew you could do it!" But the farmer and the bamboo knew all along that the growth had been happening steadily beneath the surface, even when it wasn't visible.

This story is a powerful reminder of the importance of nurturing our dreams and goals, even when we don't see immediate results. We must continue to water our dreams and practice delayed gratification. The vision of achieving something greater is given to us—not to our neighbors, friends, or family members. It is our responsibility to nurture that vision, despite the lack of immediate validation. Some things won't happen as quickly as we want them to, and many obstacles will catch us off guard. It's essential to deal with these challenges head-on as they arise, knowing that growth is often a slow, unseen process.

As Tiger Woods famously said, "Nothing is ever going to be given to you; everything is going to be earned."[1] This means that if we don't put in the work and effort, we won't get the results we desire. More importantly, we won't deserve the success. We need to earn it. The story of the Chinese bamboo tree teaches us that our consistent efforts, even when they seem fruitless, are building the foundation for future success. Patience, perseverance, and unwavering faith in our vision are the keys to achieving our dreams, and, ultimately, to seeing that bamboo shoot ninety feet into the sky.

Analysis Paralysis

Starting something new is often the most challenging part of any journey. Many of us have dreams and aspirations of achieving greater goals, yet we find ourselves stuck, unable to take that first step. This hesitation often stems from a phenomenon known as analysis paralysis—a state where overthinking and the fear of negative outcomes lead to inaction. This paralysis is born out of our desire to make the right decision, to avoid mistakes, and to ensure that every step we take is perfect. But as the famous saying goes, "Nothing worth having comes easy," and waiting for the perfect moment only leads to missed opportunities.

When we overthink, we become overwhelmed by the myriad possibilities, potential failures, and the fear of making the wrong decision. This state of confusion prevents us from moving forward. Entrepreneur and author Dr. Ivan Minser aptly describes this condition, noting that it is especially prevalent among knowledgeable individuals. These people often know exactly what they need to do to succeed, yet they remain frozen, unable to act because they are waiting for the perfect time—a time that may never come. As Dr. Minser puts it, "Ignorance on fire is way better than knowledge on ice."[2] The truth is, no one can maximize their life by making all the right decisions; it's just not possible. *Adversity is inevitable, but growth is optional.*

Overthinking and the fear of imperfection can freeze us into inaction, preventing meaningful progress. I experienced this firsthand during my freshman year when I became fascinated with entrepreneurship. I explored countless business ideas, from ATM machines and real estate to car rentals and clothing brands. Yet instead of diving into any of them, I found myself stuck, constantly researching but never acting. I felt the need to master every area before I could take meaningful steps forward. The fear of making a mistake kept me from committing to any of these pursuits.

In hindsight, while I didn't take financial risks, the experience wasn't wasted. The intense research helped me clarify my goals and build foundational skills. I developed concepts, partnerships, and business plans that would later inform my entrepreneurial pursuits. This period taught me an important lesson: Imperfect action often leads to clarity, while endless overthinking does not. Recognizing the cost of inaction, I've since learned to balance preparation with execution, trusting that progress comes from taking the first step, no matter how uncertain I feel.

The most important thing is to take that first step, even when the path ahead is unclear. Mark Zuckerberg highlighted that no one starts with fully formed ideas. Clarity comes through the process of working on an idea, not before. If he had waited to understand everything about connecting people, Facebook might never have been created. The belief in a single eureka moment is misleading and prevents people with great potential from starting. Instead, it's through taking action that ideas evolve and take shape.

There is no perfect time to start something new, to go for your dreams, or to take action. The only perfect time is now. The fear of starting, however, can be paralyzing. Kevin Hart speaks to this fear, stating that the *fear of failure often translates into a fear of starting*. People are afraid of what might go wrong, and this fear stops them before they even begin. Hart suggests embracing the side of discovery—trying things out to see what works and what doesn't. "I don't know what I'm not going to be good at until I've tried to do it,"[3] he says, emphasizing the importance of action over inaction.

Ideas are abundant, but the hardest part is turning them into reality. The biggest challenge lies in taking the first step—getting an idea out of your head and starting to build it. This process often begins by sketching out ideas, discussing them, and taking small, actionable steps to make them real. Inaction, though seemingly harmless, carries a significant cost. Our most valuable resource is not time, but attention. When our attention is consumed by worry or indecision, we miss the chance to enjoy the present moment or make progress toward our goals. Recognizing this cost can motivate us to act sooner rather than later and commit to moving forward.

The Bible also provides wisdom on this topic in Ecclesiastes 11:4: "Whoever watches the wind will not plant; whoever looks at the clouds will not reap" (NIV). It teaches us that farmers who wait for perfect weather never plant, and those who watch every cloud never harvest. This verse is a powerful reminder that waiting for the perfect conditions will only lead to missed opportunities. There will never be a perfect time to plant the seeds of our dreams; the key is to take that leap of faith regardless of the circumstances.

Steve Harvey echoes this sentiment, emphasizing that when God puts something in your imagination, you must act on it. The "how to" is not your concern; your job is to take that leap of faith and start. Harvey explains that many people trip themselves out of their blessings because they are too focused on figuring out every detail before they begin. But the truth is, you don't need to know how to make a million dollars to start working toward that goal. You just need to start. "Quit tripping yourself out of the blessing because you're worried about how to," Harvey advises.[4]

Once you've taken that first step, the next crucial factor is consistent effort and delayed gratification. The concept of delayed gratification is central to achieving any significant goal. It's the ability to resist the temptation of immediate rewards in favor of long-term gains. This mindset is crucial for anyone striving for success, as it enables us to stay focused on our long-term objectives, even when the immediate rewards are not visible. Consistent effort, day in and day out, is what ultimately leads to the achievement of these long-term goals.

The Illusion of Judgment

Another reason people hesitate to start is the fear of being judged by others. We often live our lives as if everyone around us is watching and judging our every move. This fear can be paralyzing, preventing us from taking the necessary steps toward our goals. But the truth is that most people are too consumed with their own lives to be constantly judging us. The problem lies not in the external world, but within us—our own insecurities and fears. To move forward, we must let go of this fear of judgment and focus on our own journey.

Starting is never easy. The fear of making the wrong decision, the fear of failure, and the fear of judgment can all hold us back. But as all these voices remind us, the key is to take that first step, to act even when we feel uncertain, and to trust that the path will become clearer as we move forward. The cost of inaction is far greater than the cost of making mistakes along the way. By taking action, we not only move closer to our goals, but we also build the confidence and clarity needed to continue on our journey. Failure is the price of entry, but it is also the path to growth and success.

The Importance of Consistent Effort

Achieving long-term goals requires more than just a burst of enthusiasm or a fleeting moment of motivation. It demands consistent effort, discipline, and the willingness to delay gratification. In a world that often promotes quick fixes and instant results, the value of persistent effort cannot be overstated. It's through continuous, dedicated action that we lay the groundwork for future success. Continuous action is the engine that drives long-term success. It's not enough to work hard for a short period; the real challenge is to maintain that effort consistently over time. This means showing up every day, putting in the work, and staying committed to your goals, even when the progress seems slow or invisible. It's this relentless commitment to action that separates those who achieve their goals from those who fall short.

Brian Tracy, a renowned personal development expert, emphasizes the importance of tackling the most challenging tasks first. He suggests that you should "eat the frog" first thing in the morning—meaning, start your day by doing the hardest, most unpleasant task on your list.[5] By doing this, you overcome procrastination and set a productive tone for the rest of your day. Tracy notes that people who exercise first thing in the morning are several times more likely to maintain their exercise routine compared to those who wait until later in the day. The reasoning is simple: Later in the day, it's easy to find excuses to procrastinate. By starting with the toughest task, you build momentum and make it easier to maintain consistent effort throughout the day.

In the pursuit of long-term goals, consistent effort and the ability to delay gratification are crucial. Success is not achieved overnight; it is the result of continuous action and persistent effort over time. By adopting a mindset of delayed gratification and making a habit of tackling the most challenging tasks first, we can build the discipline and resilience needed to achieve our long-term goals.

Set Clear and Meaningful Goals

One of the primary reasons people struggle to take action is because they lack clear and meaningful goals. Without a well-defined objective, it's easy to feel lost, overwhelmed, or unmotivated. Setting clear goals not only provides direction but also creates a sense of purpose and urgency that drives action. To help with this, productivity expert Brian Tracy developed the ABCDE Method, a powerful technique for prioritizing tasks and managing time effectively. It categorizes tasks based on their importance and urgency, helping individuals and teams focus on what truly matters.

- **A: Must Do**: These are your top priority tasks. They are critical to achieving your goals and must be done, no exceptions.

- **B: Should Do**: These tasks are important, but not as crucial as the "A" tasks. They should be done after you have completed your "A" tasks.

- **C: Nice to Do**: These are tasks that would be nice to complete but are not essential. They can be done if time allows, after completing both "A" and "B" tasks.

- **D: Delegate**: These tasks are important but can be handled by someone else. Delegating these tasks frees up your time to focus on the "A" tasks.

- **E: Eliminate**: These tasks are neither important nor urgent. They do not contribute to your goals and should be eliminated from your to-do list.[6]

When setting goals or making a to-do list, the first step is to categorize each task using the ABCDE Method. This helps you prioritize what needs to be done and allows you to delegate or eliminate tasks that do not contribute significantly to your objectives. For example, when planning for the next one to five years, you can list all the things you would like to accomplish and then assign each item a priority level—A, B, or C. From there, you can break down your A tasks into smaller, more manageable steps, such as A-1, A-2, and A-3, with A-1 being the most important.

Prioritizing tasks is essential for effective time management and productivity. When you know what your most important tasks are, you can focus your energy on what truly matters, rather than getting bogged down by less important activities. Setting clear goals and prioritizing tasks ensures that you stay on track and make steady progress toward your objectives. Without clear priorities, it's easy to get distracted or overwhelmed by the sheer volume of tasks that demand your attention.

The 6-Step Method for Achieving Goals

Once you've set and prioritized your goals using the ABCDE Method, the next step is to implement a process for achieving them. The 6-Step Method provides a structured approach to goal achievement:

1. **Set and Choose Your Goals:** Clearly define what you want to achieve. Be specific about your goals and write them down.
2. **Set Priorities:** Determine which goals and tasks are most important and should be tackled first.
3. **Choose Your Activities:** Identify the specific actions you need to take to achieve your goals.
4. **Set Priorities Again:** Within your chosen activities, prioritize the most important tasks to ensure you're focusing on what matters most.
5. **Schedule:** Create a timeline or schedule for completing your tasks. Set deadlines and allocate time for each activity.
6. **Implement:** Take action and start working on your tasks according to your schedule. Consistent action is key to achieving your goals.

The Value of Taking Risks

In life, taking risks is not only necessary; it's essential for growth and success. While the allure of security and stability is strong, it often comes at the cost of missed opportunities and unfulfilled potential. Risk-taking pushes us out of our comfort zones, forces us to confront our fears, and ultimately allows us to achieve things we never thought possible. The journey of life is inherently risky, and embracing this reality is crucial for personal and professional development.

Douglas MacArthur said, "There is no security on this earth; there is only opportunity."[7] Life is very perverse in a way, because the more we seek security, the less we have it, and the more we seek opportunity, the more we have security. This resonates when considering the power of risk-taking. While security may feel comforting, it often leads to stagnation, while taking risks opens the door to transformative growth. A personal example of this principle is my decision to pursue a dual degree program abroad.

As a U.S. and EU citizen with a passion for travel, I was drawn to the opportunity to earn two degrees in four years—one from my home institution in the U.S. and another from a European university in Rome,

Italy. The idea was both thrilling and daunting. After spending a year and a half building close friendships and thriving at my U.S. campus, the reality of uprooting my life to move abroad was overwhelming. I knew I wouldn't see many of the people I had grown close to for two years. Still, I took the leap, trusting that the experience would be worth the uncertainty and challenges. Living and studying in Italy not only pushed me out of my comfort zone but also allowed me to focus deeply on personal growth, explore new passions, and broaden my worldview. The rewards of taking this risk have been immeasurable, reinforcing my belief that choosing the harder path often leads to the greatest growth.

Helen Keller further elaborates on this concept by stating, "Life is either a daring adventure or nothing. Security does not exist in nature, nor do the children of men as a whole experience it. Avoiding danger is no safer in the long run than exposure."[8] This highlights that security is an illusion and that true growth comes from embracing risks. Keller emphasizes that avoiding challenges ultimately holds us back from living a meaningful life. Real success lies on the outer edge of your potential where fear, uncertainty, and doubt reside. Courage is not the absence of fear but the ability to move forward despite it. The *fear* of failure is the greatest single reason for failure in adult life. Therefore, confronting this fear head-on is necessary for true success.

Taking Risks Is Essential for Growth and Success

- If you laugh, you risk appearing foolish.
- If you weep, you risk being seen as overly sentimental.
- If you reach out to someone, you risk rejection.
- If you love, you risk not being loved in return.
- If you place your dreams before others, you risk ridicule.
- If you move forward against overwhelming odds, you risk failure.

Risk-taking is a fundamental component of growth. Yet risks must be taken because the greatest hazard in life is to risk nothing. The person who avoids risk may feel safe, but they also have nothing, do nothing, and become nothing. While they might escape suffering, pain, or embarrassment, they also miss out on the chance to learn, love, grow, or make meaningful changes. Only those who dare to take risks truly experience freedom.

Taking action is deeply intertwined with the power of perspective. When you take risks and embrace the uncertainty of outcomes, you shift how you view challenges and setbacks. A person who takes action understands that failure is not a stopping point but a step in the process of growth. This perspective helps turn what might seem like negative experiences—rejection, embarrassment, or failure—into valuable lessons. Each risk taken broadens your understanding of what's possible, and even when things don't go as planned, you gain insight into how to approach things differently.

Perspective changes when you realize that inaction carries far greater risk than trying and failing. By choosing to act, you're no longer confined by fear or the judgments of others. Instead, you focus on the possibilities of what could happen, allowing for growth and discovery. The power of perspective lies in seeing setbacks as part of the journey, understanding that progress is made not in avoiding risk, but in confronting it head-on. Taking action, therefore, not only helps you achieve your goals but also reshapes your mindset, making you resilient, adaptable, and ultimately free to live more fully.

Whether in business, relationships, or personal development, taking risks allows us to expand our horizons, learn from our experiences, and build resilience. Without risk, there is no reward. Those who avoid risks in pursuit of security often find themselves stuck in stagnation, unable to achieve their full potential. In business, for example, entrepreneurs who take calculated risks can innovate, disrupt industries, and create new opportunities for themselves and others. However, with these risks come the possibility of failure.

In relationships, taking risks can mean being vulnerable, expressing your true feelings, or making a commitment. These risks can lead to deeper connections and more meaningful relationships, but they also come with the potential for rejection or heartbreak. However, without taking these risks, the chance for genuine, fulfilling relationships is significantly diminished. In personal development, taking risks might involve stepping out of your comfort zone, trying something new, or pursuing a challenging goal. These risks help us grow, build confidence, and discover our strengths and weaknesses. Our fear of failure is the greatest obstacle to this kind of growth. Yet by facing our fears and taking risks, we push the boundaries of what we are capable of, leading to greater success and fulfillment.

Examples of Risks

- **Business Risks:** Starting a new venture, launching a product, or investing in a new market all involve significant risk. The potential for failure is high, but so is the potential for reward. Entrepreneurs who take these risks can innovate and lead in their industries.

- **Relationship Risks:** Opening up emotionally, committing to a relationship, or addressing conflicts can be risky, but these actions are essential for building strong, lasting connections. Without taking these risks, relationships can become superficial or stagnant.

- **Personal Risks:** Pursuing higher education, changing careers, or taking on new challenges requires courage and a willingness to embrace the unknown. These risks are necessary for personal growth and achieving one's full potential.

Taking risks is an inherent part of life. The pursuit of security often leads to missed opportunities and unfulfilled potential. True success requires courage—the courage to face our fears, take action, and embrace the unknown. Whether in business, relationships, or personal growth, taking risks allows us to push our boundaries, learn from our experiences, and achieve our goals. Time is limited, and the greatest risk of all is to do nothing. We must conserve our time and make the most of the opportunities we have, for they are finite and precious.

The Illusion of Perfection

One of the most significant barriers to taking action is the illusion of perfection—the false belief that there is a perfect time, perfect plan, or perfect set of circumstances that must be in place before we can begin. This mindset often traps people in a cycle of inaction, waiting for the "right moment" that never comes. The truth is, perfection is an illusion, and waiting for it only leads to procrastination and missed opportunities. The key to overcoming this trap is to take imperfect steps and learn through trial and error.

Many people delay pursuing their goals because they believe they must wait for the perfect moment. They convince themselves they need all the right conditions—whether it's more knowledge, the ideal mentor, sufficient funding, or flawless timing—before they can begin. However, the idea of a perfect moment is an illusion. In reality, waiting too long often leads to procrastination and missed opportunities. The key is to accept that the timing will never be perfect and to start anyway, taking action despite the uncertainty.

Steve Jobs, visionary entrepreneur and former CEO of Apple, reinforced this idea by stating that most people never act because they are afraid of failing.[9] He points out that the willingness to fail, to crash and burn, is what separates those who achieve their dreams from those who merely dream about them. Taking action, even when it's not perfect, is essential for turning dreams into reality.

Similarly, many people fall into the trap of waiting for the "right time" to take action, whether it's waiting for the weekend, a new season, or a milestone like graduation. This mindset often causes them to overlook the value of the present moment. The truth is, the only time we truly have is now. Dwelling on the past or fixating on the future means missing out on the opportunities that exist in the here and now. Embracing the present moment allows us to make the most of life, rather than waiting for a perfection that may never come.

Take Imperfect Steps: Learn Through Trial and Error

The solution to the illusion of perfection is to embrace imperfection and take action anyway. Steven Bartlett began his entrepreneurial journey with no knowledge, no funding, and no clear plan. He simply began by designing a website on PowerPoint using basic tools and then reached out to investors, learning as he went along. His approach was to move one small step at a time, understanding that each imperfect step brought him closer to his goal.

By changing the timeline for decision-making—from taking a week to make a decision to making decisions in a day—you can move through life at a much faster rate. Speed in decision-making and action can lead to exponential growth and success. By taking imperfect action now, rather than waiting for the perfect moment, you can achieve far more in a shorter amount of time. When you have nothing to lose, you should be the most prone to taking action. Starting when you have little or nothing going for you allows you to be underestimated and take endless shots on goal. This is a powerful advantage, as there's nothing holding you back from trying, learning, and growing.

The Cost of Inaction

Inaction carries a cost—a cost that is often underestimated or ignored. The tendency to delay, procrastinate, or wait for the perfect conditions can lead to missed opportunities, unfulfilled potential, and, ultimately, regret. Recognizing the value of acting sooner rather than later is crucial for avoiding the high price of inaction. We often presume inaction has no cost, but this is a dangerous misconception. The most important resource we have in life is not time, but attention. Time can pass unnoticed when our attention is captured by distractions, worries, or indecision. By contemplating the price we pay for inaction, we can better understand the importance of doing things sooner rather than later and committing to our goals.

Time wasted is *time wasted*. It is gone forever. You can always make back ten dollars, but you'll never get back ten minutes once they're gone. Prioritize your time over money. Years spent thinking about going to the gym won't get you in shape. Thinking about starting a business won't make you rich. Thinking about launching a YouTube channel won't get you views or money. Your time on this planet is limited, so ask yourself: Am I going to spend half my life just thinking about it, or am I going to take action and start right now? Just do it.

Time is a finite resource, and it's easy to fall into the illusion that we have more of it than we actually do. A simple way to grasp this reality is to break it down into tangible examples. For instance, if you take one family vacation each year and assume you have forty years left, you don't have forty years of vacations—you only have forty more trips with your loved ones. Thinking in these terms highlights the urgency of taking action now rather than postponing it. Every moment of inaction is a moment lost forever, reminding us to make the most of the time we have.

In business, inaction can mean the difference between seizing a market opportunity and watching it pass by. Entrepreneurs who hesitate to launch a product, enter a new market, or make a bold decision may find that the

opportunity is no longer available when they finally decide to act. The same applies in personal relationships, where failing to express feelings, make a commitment, or resolve conflicts can lead to missed chances for deep connection and fulfillment.

In personal growth, inaction often results in stagnation. The fear of failure, the desire for perfection, or the illusion of endless time can prevent people from pursuing their dreams, learning new skills, or taking on challenges that would lead to personal development. As a result, they may look back with regret, realizing that the opportunities they once had are no longer available.

Building Confidence Through Action

Confidence is often misunderstood as an innate personality trait, something you either have or don't. However, the truth is that confidence is a skill—one that can be developed and strengthened through action. The more you move from thought to action, the more your self-belief grows, and the more confident you become in your abilities. This section explores how taking action builds confidence and provides insights from various influential figures on overcoming the fear of failure.

Confidence is not something you are born with; it is something you acquire through experience and action. When you start to see confidence as a skill rather than a personality trait, it becomes clear that anyone can develop it. Confidence is the ability to move from thought to action. When you believe in yourself and your capabilities enough to try, you start building the confidence that leads to greater success. By taking steps, even small ones, you reinforce your belief in your ability to handle challenges, which in turn, builds more confidence.

This idea resonates deeply with my experience in martial arts. During my freshman year of college, I discovered a judo and jiu-jitsu class on campus. Having developed a fascination with martial arts during my senior year of high school, I immediately signed up. This decision became one of the most empowering steps I've taken thus far. Each class tested my physical and mental limits, pushing me to embrace discomfort and trust in my abilities.

Over time, I saw myself improve—not just in technique but also in how I approached challenges in life. Martial arts taught me that showing up consistently and committing to action builds both strength and self-belief. It reinforced my confidence in following through with decisions and trusting my instincts. This lesson has stayed with me, serving as a reminder that confidence isn't innate; it's built through action and perseverance.

The paralysis of overthinking often stems from the belief that we need to make the perfect decision before taking action. However, clarity doesn't come from endless deliberation—it comes from action. Each step forward provides more insight, revealing the path as we go. This trial-and-error process is essential for building both confidence and momentum, proving that progress is made by doing, not just thinking. Kobe Bryant, known for his relentless work ethic, provides a simple yet profound insight: "The best way to prove your value is to work, to learn, to absorb, to be a sponge."[10] For Bryant, confidence was built not through innate talent but through consistent action and a willingness to outwork his potential. Emotions come and go, but what's important is how you choose to respond to them. By stepping back, analyzing your fears, and taking action despite them, you can control your emotions rather than being controlled by them. This approach to fear and action is integral to building confidence.

> "The heaviest things in life aren't iron or gold, but
> unmade decisions. The reason you are stressed is that
> you have decisions to make, and you're not making them."
> —Chris Williamson

Overcoming Self-Doubt

Self-doubt is a major obstacle to taking action and building confidence. It often stems from past failures, unmet promises to oneself, or the fear of judgment. Overcoming self-doubt requires a commitment to yourself, a belief in your own abilities, and the willingness to take action despite the fear. Self-belief is critical in overcoming self-doubt. Many people don't move forward because they haven't stood by the promises they've made to themselves. Every time you break a promise to yourself, you chip away at your confidence. Self-belief is built through consistency—by doing what you say you're going to do, even when it's difficult. This consistency reinforces your confidence and diminishes self-doubt.

Self-encouragement can deflect doubt and push you to keep going, even when it feels like the world is against you. One key perspective is to stop dwelling on limitations and start believing in your potential. By toughening up and becoming someone the world needs, you shift from passive doubt to active progress. Believing in yourself like you believe in your role models—whether they are celebrities, athletes, or other figures—can inspire you to keep going, even when times are tough. This relentless self-encouragement is key to overcoming self-doubt and achieving your goals. The journey to achieving your dreams and goals begins with a single step. It's easy to get caught up in planning, perfectionism, or fear, but the only way to make progress is to start. Whether that step is big or small, perfect or imperfect, it's the beginning of a path that leads to growth, learning, and success. Remember, as many of the voices in this discussion have emphasized, the key is to act now, to embrace the journey, and to trust that with each step, you are building the life you envision.

"Inaction breeds doubt and fear. Action breeds confidence and courage." —Dale Carnegie

14
The Price of Progress

The concept of "price" touches every aspect of life—whether it's physical fitness, education, relationships, or personal growth. We constantly trade our time, effort, and energy to gain traits like toughness or patience. To grow tougher, one must endure hardship. To develop patience, we must resist the temptation of immediate gratification. Each desired quality has a cost, a metaphorical price tag, and understanding this trade-off helps us appreciate the value of the experiences we endure.

The price of progress often tests the alignment between our actions and our inner compass. While striving for growth, success, or achievement, we can find ourselves at crossroads where the pursuit of progress demands sacrifices—our time, energy, relationships, or even our values. If we ignore the quiet pull of our inner compass during these moments, the cost of progress can feel hollow, leaving us unfulfilled despite outward gains.

We must also be aware of uncertainty in our pursuits. If success were guaranteed, the process would lose its meaning. The journey itself—the struggle, growth, and transformation—carries the most value. Ancient Greeks believed the gods envied mortals for their uncertain, ever-changing lives. This unpredictability is what gives human experiences their depth and meaning. To thrive, we must embrace the struggles and uncertainties as integral to personal growth.

In my own life, jiu-jitsu has been one of the most vivid illustrations of paying the price for growth. I started training in January 2024 as a white belt, knowing I would face countless losses. Each session meant showing up to be submitted repeatedly by higher belts—blue, purple, brown, or black. The effort of packing my bag, traveling to the gym, and enduring two hours of consistent defeat was daunting. Yet these challenges taught me invaluable lessons about resilience, humility, and the importance of embracing discomfort.

> *"If you think the price of winning is too high, wait until you get the bill from regret."* —Tim Grover

The physical demands of jiu-jitsu were just as significant. Soreness, injuries, and mental fatigue were constant companions. Training required sacrificing nights out with friends and rest days to remain consistent. But these sacrifices were the price I willingly paid for the discipline and mental toughness that came with the art. In every session, I had a choice: Let the losses discourage me, or use them as fuel to grow stronger. I chose the harder path, finding fulfillment in each challenge I overcame.

This same principle applies to other forms of physical fitness. Running half-marathons, for example, demands hours of preparation and conditioning. The time and effort invested in training were the price of crossing the finish line and experiencing the profound sense of accomplishment that came with it. Enduring discomfort strengthens us and reinforces our purpose.

The concept of *price* extends beyond physical fitness into other areas of life. Pursuing dual degrees from institutions in both America and Europe required me to navigate the challenges of different academic systems, time zones, and cultures. It meant sacrificing time with friends and adapting to relationships stretched across continents. As I plan to attend law school in the near future, I anticipate the demands of countless hours of study, preparation for exams, and prioritizing academics over social events and hobbies. These experiences reflect the reality that success often requires trading short-term gratification for long-term achievements.

Learning new skills carries a similar cost. Achieving conversational fluency in a new language, for instance, required sacrificing time spent on less meaningful activities, like scrolling through social media. Instead, I invested in consistent practice and disciplined effort. While progress felt slow at first, the payoff came in the form of enriched future opportunities and a broadened perspective. Gratefully, traveling to over eighty countries has been one of the most rewarding—and costly—endeavors of my life. Financially, emotionally, and logistically, the price was steep. I've never lived in one place for more than two years, which has meant continually leaving behind comfort zones and close friendships. Each move required me to start over, both socially and emotionally. But this cost yielded life-changing perspectives, exposing me to new cultures and ideas that have profoundly shaped my worldview. Growth often demands that we leave behind the familiar to embrace the unknown.

Relationships also come with their own price. Frequent moves forced me to choose between maintaining shallow connections and investing in deeper, more fulfilling relationships. Recognizing this trade-off early on allowed me to focus on the latter. Prioritizing quality over quantity has helped me nurture bonds that align with my values, even when distance posed challenges. On a broader level, the price of personal growth often involves facing discomfort and rejection. For instance, choosing delayed gratification over emotional reactions builds a stable, long-term mindset. Developing emotional intelligence has been crucial in maintaining perspective during challenging times. Reflecting on setbacks and understanding their value has helped me grow stronger and more resilient.

Faith has also been a guiding force through these trials. As a freshman in college, uncertain about where to begin my entrepreneurial journey, I turned to faith for guidance. This decision gave me the courage to choose harder paths, seek mentors, and challenge my beliefs. Leaning into discomfort—whether by asking hard questions or confronting doubts—helped me develop a deeper sense of purpose and prioritize spiritual growth over material pursuits.

These lessons manifest in practical ways. Budgeting time and energy is critical. Prioritizing long-term goals, like career advancement, often requires cutting back on immediate indulgences. Financially, this might mean investing in courses or fitness programs rather than impulsive luxuries. Mentally, it means dedicating time to activities with the greatest return on growth, such as building meaningful skills or relationships.

Setbacks are part of the cost too. Failures can be reframed as necessary payments for success. Moving to a new country without knowing the language, pivoting careers, or publicly sharing creative work all come with uncertainty. Yet these risks also hold the potential for transformation. The rewards may not come immediately, but the act of taking these steps builds resilience and courage.

Failure is the price of entry.

Ultimately, the price of growth—whether physical, mental, or emotional—is the currency of progress. Recognizing and embracing this cost cultivates the resilience and perspective needed to achieve meaningful goals. Life's unpredictability is what makes it valuable. By appreciating the journey with all its struggles and triumphs, we unlock our potential and find fulfillment in the process.

15
The Love of Learning
First Be a Student,
Then a Teacher

Self-improvement is not just a goal; it is a way of life. It requires us to embrace a mindset of continuous growth, fueled by curiosity, resilience, and an unrelenting desire to become better each day. In this chapter, we will explore the transformative power of learning and the principles that enable personal growth. From mastering the art of teachability to understanding the value of shared vision, mentoring, and intentional action, the journey of self-improvement invites us to challenge our beliefs, refine our habits, and inspire others along the way. By cultivating these values, we not only enrich our own lives but also create a ripple effect that impacts those around us. The path forward is not always easy, but it is profoundly rewarding—an ongoing process of growth that strengthens character, sharpens perspective, and brings clarity to the purpose we each hold.

Learning and self-improvement are at the heart of a fulfilling life. This chapter delves into the principles and philosophies that can guide us on our journey to becoming the best version of ourselves. From the wisdom of ancient philosophers to contemporary insights, these lessons underscore the importance of embracing challenges, cultivating gratitude, and staying true to oneself. Through stories, quotes, and practical advice, this chapter aims to inspire a lifelong love of learning and a deeper appreciation for the nuances of personal growth.

> *"As a society, we must teach what is taught to advance future generations."*

Once we train ourselves to remain open-minded and teachable, we not only acquire new skills and insights but also develop the wisdom to guide and mentor others. The process of learning transforms us, equipping us with the empathy, patience, and understanding required to inspire growth in those around us. By remaining teachable, we set a foundation for lifelong improvement, allowing us to share what we've learned and help others navigate their own journeys. In doing so, the act of teaching and mentoring becomes an extension of our own learning process, creating a cycle of growth that benefits both ourselves and those we mentor. But it all begins with the willingness to remain teachable.

The Value of Remaining Open-Minded and Teachable

Teachability is defined as being "able and willing to learn" and is a fundamental trait that drives both personal and professional growth. It involves humility, the ability to embrace constructive criticism, and an openness to learn from anyone, regardless of their background or status. This mindset fosters adaptability, which is essential for navigating the complexities of modern life and work. In a world where change is constant, those who cultivate teachability gain a significant advantage, as they are better equipped to adapt to new challenges and seize opportunities for growth.

A teachable person is characterized by their ability to receive feedback without defensiveness, acknowledge mistakes without excuses, and actively seek to understand others' viewpoints through clarifying questions. These attributes help individuals remain open to new ideas and challenge their own assumptions and perceptions, allowing them to grow and improve continuously. The process of maintaining a teachable spirit is not passive—it requires deliberate effort and intentionality. This includes reflecting on past experiences, seeking feedback from others, and actively engaging with new perspectives. Leaders, in particular, benefit immensely from teachability, as it allows them to inspire collaboration, empower their teams, and model a growth-oriented mindset for others.

Teachability is not confined to individual growth; it extends to teams and organizations. Groups that prioritize open-mindedness create environments where critical thinking and innovative problem-solving thrive. Research highlights the importance of task-oriented cognitive conflict, a constructive form of disagreement that encourages diverse perspectives and critical reflection. This type of conflict supports deeper learning and prevents groupthink by challenging assumptions and broadening the range of ideas considered in decision-making processes. Such an environment not only enhances the learning capacity of groups, but also leads to better outcomes in terms of creativity and adaptability.

The concept of lifelong learning underscores the value of teachability in today's rapidly evolving job landscape. Unlike previous generations, where individuals often remained in a single job or career throughout their lives, modern professionals frequently change roles and industries. This dynamic demands an ongoing commitment to learning and adaptability. Lifelong learning is not just a professional necessity, but also a source of personal fulfillment, as it promotes curiosity and resilience in the face of change. Flexible educational models, such as online learning platforms and accelerated skill-building programs, demonstrate how teachability can be supported in practical ways. These platforms allow individuals to acquire new skills while continuing to work, showcasing the power of open-mindedness in achieving personal and professional goals.

Mentoring relationships also illustrate the profound impact of teachability. Mentees who approach these relationships with an open mind gain life skills, confidence, and new perspectives, while mentors themselves benefit from the opportunity to reflect, learn, and grow through their interactions with mentees. This reciprocal learning dynamic highlights how teachability can reinforce mutual improvement and collaboration, strengthening both individuals and communities. Research shows that mentoring relationships thrive when both parties are willing to listen, adapt, and embrace the learning process. Long-term mentoring connections, built on trust and openness, yield significant benefits for both mentors and mentees, including improved self-esteem, stronger interpersonal skills, and greater resilience.[1]

Teachability is also essential for cultivating shared vision and collective learning in organizations. Open-mindedness ensures that groups are able to critically assess their goals, beliefs, and strategies, allowing them to adapt to changing circumstances and achieve common objectives. Shared vision, when combined with teachability, strengthens group cohesion and motivation, creating a powerful dynamic that drives collective success. However, this balance must be carefully maintained to avoid rigidity or conformity, which can stifle innovation and critical thinking.

Use the Power of Words to Alter Your Perspective

- "They hurt me, so I'll make sure they feel my pain."
  - *No, nobody deserves that kind of pain.*
- "Everyone is so much better than me."
  - *I'll become the best version of myself.*
- "I wish I could go back and change things."
  - *Everything was a lesson and was necessary.*
- "I'm so tired. I want to give up."
  - *Everybody's tired. This is where I separate myself.*

- "I shouldn't have done that."
  - *I needed that lesson in order to grow.*
- "Everyone is so much better than me."
  - *I'm not in competition with anybody.*
- "Why is this happening to me?"
  - *What is this trying to teach me?*
- "It's too late for me to start."
  - *Every moment is a new opportunity.*
- "Nobody understands me."
  - *I understand myself, and that's enough.*
- "I give up. It's hopeless."
  - *As long as I keep trying, there is hope.*
- "I have no motivation. I will do what I have to do."
  - *I don't need motivation. I'll do what I have to do.*

Study Tips for Effective Learning

Effective learning isn't just about working harder; it's about working smarter. Incorporating proven strategies can enhance your understanding, retention, and productivity. The following are a few powerful methods that can transform your study habits.

Teach to Learn:
- Simplify complex concepts by explaining them to someone else. This forces you to break down ideas into manageable parts and identify any gaps in your understanding.

Active Recall:
- Test your memory by writing down everything you know about a topic from memory. This process strengthens retention and highlights areas that need more focus.

Review Regularly:

- o Reinforce what you've learned by revisiting it at spaced intervals over time. This approach prevents forgetting and strengthens long-term memory.

Time Efficiency:

- o Set clear, tight deadlines for tasks. This helps prevent procrastination and ensures you stay focused, as work tends to expand to fill the time available.

Organized Notes:

- o Store information externally using tools like written notes or digital systems. This "second brain" system declutters your mind and enhances creativity by making information accessible when needed.

Optimize Energy:

- o Schedule tasks around your natural energy levels throughout the day. By aligning your work with when you feel most alert, you can study more effectively.

Backwards Law (Alan Watts)

Alan Watts calls this the "backwards law", also known as the law of reverse effort: The more you try, the further away you are. For example, the more you try to float, the more you sink. In dating, the harder you chase someone, the faster they run away, sensing your desperation. Regarding money, the more you stress about not having it, the more you fall into a scarcity mentality, closing your own doors.[2]

Confidence isn't about cockiness or arrogance; it's about intense trust in yourself. True confidence comes from a deep-seated belief that you are capable and can make things happen. The secret to gaining more confidence is to stop trying and to start trusting yourself. Trust in your capabilities, and watch your confidence and success increase.

Wisdom and Reflections

- Seneca: "We suffer more in our imagination than in reality."[3]
- George Eliot: "It's never too late to be what you might have been."[4]
- Marcus Aurelius: "Our life is what our thoughts make it."[5]
- Carl Jung: "Thinking is difficult; that's why most people judge."[6]
- Lao Tzu: "Care about what other people think and you will always be their prisoner."[7]
- Pythagoras: "A fool is known by his speech and a wise man by silence."[8]
- Confucius: "If you are the smartest person in the room, then you are in the wrong room."[9]
- Rumi: "The quieter you become, the more you are able to hear."[10]

How Successful Learners Approach Skill Development

- Commit to the Process:
  Developing a skill takes consistent time and effort. Adopting the mindset of persistence and dedication ensures steady progress, even when results aren't immediate.
- Accept Discomfort:
  Growth often involves stepping outside your comfort zone. Embracing discomfort as a natural part of the learning journey prevents stagnation and accelerates development.
- Learn from Mistakes:
  Mistakes are not failures; they are opportunities to refine your approach and deepen your understanding. Viewing them as valuable lessons transforms setbacks into progress.

Value Feedback:

- Seeking constructive feedback and guidance from others is essential. Honest input, whether from mentors, peers, or coaches, helps identify blind spots and provides new strategies for improvement.

The Value of Shared Vision and Group Learning

Shared vision and group learning are powerful drivers of collective growth and success. A shared vision serves as a unifying force, aligning individuals and teams toward a common purpose. This alignment inspires cohesion, motivation, and clarity, enabling groups to work collaboratively to achieve their goals. When group members share a common sense of purpose, they create an environment where contributions are valued and collective efforts are amplified. Research highlights that shared vision is essential for learning-oriented environments, as it provides the direction and energy necessary to overcome obstacles and maintain focus on long-term objectives.

Group learning, on the other hand, thrives in environments where collaboration and the exchange of ideas are encouraged. Organizations that prioritize shared learning opportunities empower individuals to contribute their unique perspectives while benefiting from the collective knowledge of the group. This process not only enhances decision-making but also reinforces a culture of innovation and adaptability. When teams engage in reflective dialogues and constructive debates, they are better able to challenge assumptions, identify solutions, and implement effective strategies. Shared vision strengthens this process by aligning group members' efforts and ensuring that their learning remains purposeful and goal-oriented.

The role of mentorship also underscores the importance of shared vision in fostering group learning. Mentoring relationships often involve a clear understanding of mutual goals, whether related to professional development, personal growth, or academic achievement. This alignment creates a strong foundation for collaboration, where mentors and mentees work together toward shared objectives. Mentoring programs can significantly enhance participants' educational outcomes, interpersonal skills, and overall motivation by creating a supportive environment where shared learning is prioritized. These programs encourage collaboration among mentees, mentors, and their broader communities, further reinforcing the value of shared vision in achieving meaningful outcomes.

In professional settings, shared vision is often tied to training and development programs that emphasize group learning. For example, organizations that invest in skill-building initiatives not only enhance individual capabilities, but also strengthen the overall performance of their teams. These programs create a sense of purpose and unity, motivating employees to engage in continuous learning and contributing to collective success. Additionally, shared vision ensures that learning efforts are aligned with organizational goals, maximizing the impact of training and development initiatives. Employees who participate in such programs report higher job satisfaction and a greater sense of fulfillment, highlighting the value of collective growth.

Group learning also benefits from constructive conflict, which encourages members to share diverse perspectives and challenge each other's ideas. Task-oriented conflict, when managed effectively, can enhance group dynamics by facilitating critical thinking and innovation. This type of conflict prevents groupthink and promotes deeper engagement with complex issues, leading to more effective decision-making. Shared vision plays a crucial role in ensuring that such conflict remains productive, as it keeps the group focused on common goals and prevents personal disagreements from undermining the learning process.

Furthermore, shared vision and group learning create a ripple effect that extends beyond the immediate group. As individuals internalize the values and goals of their teams, they are more likely to share their knowledge and experiences with others, contributing to a broader culture of learning. For example, in mentoring programs, mentors often become ambassadors for the shared vision, inspiring others to engage in similar relationships and expand the reach of collective growth. Similarly, organizations that emphasize group learning often see their employees applying shared knowledge to new challenges, inspiring a continuous cycle of improvement and innovation.

The Dance of Life: Wisdom from Alan Watts

Alan Watts, philosopher, speaker, and author, believed that the meaning and purpose of dancing lie in the dance itself, similar to how music finds fulfillment in each moment of its course. One does not play a sonata just to reach the final chord; it's about experiencing each note along the way. If the value were solely in the ending, composers would only write finales.

He imagined life as a dance, suggesting that life, like a dance, should be enjoyed in each moment rather than rushing to the end. People often focus too much on reaching their goals and forget to appreciate the journey.

The essence of his message is that the journey itself is the destination, emphasizing the importance of being present and fully engaged in each moment.[11]

Ethical Guidance

Dave Chappelle said, "People are trying to replace the ideas of *good* and *bad* with *better* or *worse*, and that is incorrect. You gotta keep your ethics intact, because good and bad is a compass that helps you find the way, and a person that only does what's better or worse is the easiest type of person to control. They are a mouse in a maze that just finds the cheese, but the one who knows about good and bad will realize he's in a maze."[12]

Time Management and Life Choices

Steven Bartlett talks of the Roulette Table of Life: When we wake up in the morning we have twenty-four chips, representing the twenty-four hours in a day. We've already spent roughly eight of them sleeping, so we're left with around sixteen chips to place on the roulette table of life. This metaphorical roulette wheel spins every day, showing the returns based on how we placed our chips, ultimately deciding the outcome of our lives. The fundamental lesson is that how we place these chips is how we use our time, which is our most valuable currency.[13]

The Power of Small Actions

One minute can change an hour, an hour can change a day, one day can change a week, one week can change a month, one month can change a year, and a year can change your entire life. These actions might seem small right now, but they're part of something bigger. Those actions will build or rebuild your life or destroy it.

Cultivating a Teachable Spirit

Cultivating a teachable spirit is an intentional and ongoing process that empowers personal and professional growth. A teachable spirit involves humility, curiosity, and the willingness to embrace new ideas and feedback. It is not merely a mindset, but a practice that must be actively developed through self-reflection, engagement with others, and a commitment to continuous improvement. Individuals with a teachable spirit are open to learning from anyone, whether through mentorship, group interactions, or personal experiences. This openness allows them to remain adaptable and resilient in the face of challenges and change.

Daily intentionality is central to cultivating a teachable spirit. Much like tending a garden, personal growth requires consistent effort, including reflection on past experiences, identifying lessons, and seeking opportunities to learn. Setting growth as a priority ensures that individuals remain focused on improving themselves and their abilities. By asking questions, seeking feedback, and embracing constructive criticism, they unlock new insights and refine their understanding of the word. Reflection and critical self-assessment are particularly vital, as they encourage individuals to examine their assumptions and beliefs, leading to deeper self-awareness and adaptability.

In professional contexts, a teachable spirit translates into better engagement with training and development opportunities. Employees who approach learning with curiosity and an open mind often derive the most benefit from these programs, not only enhancing their skills, but also contributing to their organization's success. Flexible and accessible learning models, such as online platforms, make it easier for individuals to integrate education into their lives, empowering a culture of lifelong learning. These platforms cater to the needs of working professionals, enabling them to acquire new skills while maintaining their existing responsibilities. Such tools emphasize the importance of staying teachable in a rapidly evolving job market, where the ability to learn and adapt is increasingly valuable.

A teachable spirit also thrives in environments that encourage constructive conflict and dialogue. Groups that engage in open discussions and welcome diverse viewpoints create opportunities for individual and collective learning. By embracing task-oriented conflict, individuals challenge their assumptions and expand their perspectives, ultimately refining their skills and knowledge. Such environments promote a culture of inquiry and reflection, where the focus is on finding solutions rather than assigning blame. This aligns closely with the principles of double-loop learning, which emphasizes the need to question existing frameworks and explore new possibilities.

Seven Habits That Are Hard to Do, but Will Pay Off Forever

Delaying Gratification:
Your ability to delay gratification determines your success. Trust the process and give it time, like a seed growing into a plant.

Breaking Procrastination:
Overthinking, overplanning, and overanalyzing hinder progress. Shorten the gap between idea and action to level up.

Saying No:
Set clear boundaries and stick to them. A full-hearted no is better than a halfhearted yes.

Fixing Your Sleep:
Quality sleep is crucial. Tips: no screens in bed, body scan meditation, keep the room cool, dark, and quiet, invest in a good mattress and pillow, avoid caffeine after noon, and no food two hours before bed.

Facing Fear:
Don't let fear hold you back. Sign up for that class, build that business, put yourself out there. Those who mind don't matter, and those who matter don't mind.

Being Consistent:
Consistency is key. It's easy to start, but can you maintain healthy habits, workouts, or work commitments every day for years? Consistency separates doers from dreamers.

Seeking Feedback:
Learn to accept and apply criticism. Mastering this will accelerate your growth exponentially.

Avoid These Mistakes

Not Delaying Gratification:
Success takes time. Focus on consistent work and patience instead of quick results.

Following the Crowd:
Prioritize your future over current popularity. Build your own path.

Choosing What Is Easy:
Leverage your energy and freedom. Embrace challenges for personal growth.

Telling Everyone Your Plans:
Keep goals private. Work silently, and let success speak for itself.

Ignoring Your Health:
Aim for long-term success by staying physically and mentally sharp.

Stopping Your Education:
Continue learning and developing new skills even after formal education.

Not Having a Routine:
Maintain effective time management with structured routines for personal and professional growth.

Josh Kaufman: Unlock the Power of Learning Anything in Twenty Hours

You can learn any skill in just twenty hours. Whether it's a new language, drawing, or juggling flaming chainsaws, twenty hours of focused, deliberate practice is all it takes. You'll be amazed at how good you can become. Twenty hours is manageable—about forty-five minutes a day for a month, even with a few skipped days. Shifting your perspective to see learning as achievable in small, consistent efforts can transform how you approach acquiring new skills.[14]

Life Lessons by Age Twenty

Privacy is Power:
Life is better when no one knows anything about you.

Mind Your Own Business:
Peace comes from focusing on yourself.

Selective Advice:
Don't take advice from those who aren't where you want to be.

Keep Moving Forward:
Life doesn't wait; push through every day.

Don't Force Choices:
Never force anyone to choose you.

Master Your Emotions:
A calm mind can handle any situation.

Accept People as They Are:
Avoid disappointment by taking people for who they are.

Give People Time:
Everyone reveals their true self eventually.

Self-Care Is Crucial:
Take good care of yourself; the world moves on without you.

Work Hard:
Nobody cares; improve yourself daily.

Build Your Dreams:
If you don't, someone else will hire you to build theirs.

Ignore Society's Advice:
Most people have no idea what they're doing.

Create Opportunities:
Be smart enough to create your own chances; don't wait for them.

The Value of Mentoring and Being a Mentor

Mentoring holds transformative power for both mentees and mentors, creating a dynamic relationship that fosters growth, development, and mutual learning. The supportive and healthy relationships formed through mentoring contribute to numerous immediate and long-term benefits, making it a cornerstone for personal and professional success. For mentees, mentoring offers guidance, knowledge, and encouragement, while mentors gain fulfillment, improved skills, and new perspectives. These reciprocal relationships highlight the profound impact of mentorship in shaping individuals and communities. Mentors also guide us in recognizing when to say no to people, projects, or decisions that don't align with our inner compass.

Mentoring provides a wealth of benefits that span educational, behavioral, and social-emotional dimensions. Research has shown that mentees often experience improved academic performance, higher high school graduation rates, and increased college enrollment. Additionally, they exhibit healthier relationships, better decision-making, and enhanced self-esteem.[15] Programs like Big Brothers Big Sisters (BBBS) and Across Ages demonstrate how structured mentorship can reduce negative behaviors such as substance abuse and violence while enhancing stronger interpersonal skills and resilience. Mentees also gain the invaluable ability to navigate life transitions, supported by a trusted guide who offers wisdom and encouragement through challenges.

Mentors, on the other hand, experience their own set of transformative benefits. Mentoring provides a sense of accomplishment and purpose, as mentors see their efforts directly contributing to another person's growth. This role also enhances their self-esteem and helps them develop skills such as patience, leadership, and improved communication. Mentors often gain insight into the lives and challenges of younger generations, expanding their understanding and enriching their own perspectives. By modeling teachability and a growth mindset, mentors not only impart valuable lessons, but also reinforce these qualities within themselves.

Patience

Don't rush the process. Good things come to those who wait; this isn't a sprint, it's a marathon. Worrying about the future only makes you lose sight of the present. You need to get up, put one foot in front of the other, and have blind faith. We don't know when it's happening, but we must believe whole heartedly that it's coming. We're not working hard for nothing. Keep grinding.

Bearing Life's Burden

Carry the world. Pick up the world on your shoulders and walk forward. Embrace its troubles, suffering, and evil, and move forward with it. In bearing that burden, discover that you are the kind of creature capable of carrying it and deserving of respect. There is terrible evil and suffering, seemingly bottomless, but the human spirit can voluntarily take it on as a challenge.

Reframe Your Language

Instead of: Fake it until you make it.
     SAY: Act like you are.

Instead of: I can't.
     ASK: How can I?

Instead of: I have to.
     USE: I get to.

Instead of: I'm too busy.
     SAY: I'll prioritize what's important.

Instead of: I'm afraid of failing.
     SAY: I'm excited to learn from this experience.

Instead of: I'm not ready.
     SAY: I'm preparing myself.

Instead of: I'll try.
     SAY: I will.

Take Action Toward Self-Improvement

Ideal Self vs. Real Self: Once you stop fantasizing about the ideal version of yourself and start working towards becoming that person without procrastinating, you'll realize that it was simple all along. Becoming your ideal self will only ever exist in your mind until you make the decision to become that person. The difference between who you are and who you want to be is what you do.

Five Things to Know Between Ages Twenty and Fifty-Five

Take Care of Your Body
Health is another form of wealth.

Walk Some Paths Alone
Normalize walking some paths alone, because everyone has different goals.

Have Zero Expectations of Others
For happiness, keep your expectations of others at zero.

Exhibit Emotional Maturity
Exercise control over your emotions.

Free Yourself from Society's Advice
Most people have no idea what they're doing. Follow your own path.

Twenty-Three Positive Acronyms for Success

F . E . A . R
Forget Everything and Run   *or*   Face Everything and Rise

F . A . I . L
First Attempt in Learning

E . N . D
Effort Never Dies

N . O
Next Opportunity

H . O . P . E
Hold On, Pain Ends

D . R . E . A . M
Dedication, Responsibility, Education, Attitude, Motivation

P . O . W . E . R
Potential, Opportunity, Willpower, Energy, Resilience

S . M . I . L . E
Simple Moments In Life Everyday

P . A . S . S
Positive Attitude Secures Success

A . C . T
Action Changes Things

B . E . L . I . E . V . E
Because Everything Leads Invariably to Victory Eventually

G . R . O . W . T . H
Gradually Realizing Opportunities With Time and Hard work

A . C . H . I . E . V . E
Action, Commitment, Hard work, Integrity, Enthusiasm, Vision, Excellence

S.U.C.C.E.S.S
See Your Goal, Understand the Obstacles, Create a Positive Mental Picture, Clear Your Mind of Doubts, Embrace the Challenge, Stay on Track, Show the World You Can Do It

F.O.C.U.S
Follow One Course Until Successful

T.E.A.M
Together Everyone Achieves More

P.O.S.I.T.I.V.E
Persistence, Optimism, Strength, Integrity, Trust, Intuition, Vision, Enthusiasm

L.E.A.D.E.R
Listen, Engage, Act, Develop, Empower, Reflect

F.L.O.W
Focus, Let go, Optimize, Win

P.A.T.H
Plan, Action, Tenacity, Hope

G.R.I.T
Growth, Resilience, Instinct, Tenacity

S.T.R.I.V.E
Set Targets, Reach, Inspire, Value Effort

D.A.R.E
Dream, Achieve, Reflect, Excel

The journey of self-improvement is as much about learning from others as it is about teaching ourselves to adapt, persevere, and grow. Each step forward brings new insights, challenges old perceptions, and unveils the power of resilience. By remaining open-minded and teachable, we embrace the wisdom of the past, the opportunities of the present, and the potential of the future. The lessons shared here are not just ideas, but tools for navigating life's complexities with purpose and intention. Remember, growth is not about perfection; it is about progress. It is about striving to be better than we were yesterday while empowering others to do the same. As you move forward, let the principles in this chapter serve as a compass, guiding you toward a life filled with meaning, growth, and fulfillment. Keep learning, keep teaching, and keep inspiring; the person you are becoming is a testament to the journey you've embraced.

16
The Silent Mentor
Crafting a Winning Circle

Living alone in Rome, Italy, for two consecutive years has given me ample time to reflect on my circle and who I choose to interact with. Much of my time has been devoted to learning valuable skills and expanding my self-proclaimed title of being a polymath. Consequently, I spend most of my time with people who share similar productive goals—at the gym, in business, and at school. While this period of solitude has allowed me to accomplish and learn many things, I am thankful for the power of social media, which enables me to stay in touch with friends from various stages of my life.

It's important to surround yourself with individuals who challenge and inspire you. Whether it's at the gym, on the mat, or in academic settings, I've learned that being around people who are better than me—whether they're more skilled, more knowledgeable, or more disciplined—has forced me to grow. I've worked to remove the "Negative Nellies" from my life, those who drain energy or limit ambition. This has allowed me to build a supportive network of people who share their wins, encourage my growth, and inspire me to push further.

The importance of environment in shaping how we are perceived cannot be overstated. A powerful example of this comes from a 2007 social experiment. In 2007, as part of a social experiment conducted by *The Washington Post*, world-renowned violinist Joshua Bell performed incognito in the Washington, D.C., Metro station at L'Enfant Plaza. Despite playing on his $3.5 million Stradivarius and delivering classical masterpieces for forty-five minutes, Bell went largely unnoticed, collecting just $32.17 in tips from passersby. This was in stark contrast to his sold-out concert days earlier at Boston Symphony Hall, where tickets were priced in the hundreds or even thousands of dollars. The experiment highlighted how context and environment drastically affect how talent is perceived, illustrating that even the most extraordinary individuals can be overlooked in the wrong setting.[1]

> *The environment you tolerate will shape the future you create.*

This principle extends to the people you surround yourself with. Context matters. Just as Bell's brilliance went unnoticed in the wrong setting, your potential can be stifled if you're surrounded by people who don't recognize or nurture your abilities. Alex Lieberman, in his article "Why Surrounding Yourself With the Right People Is the Key to Success," underscores this point. Success, he argues, is rarely achieved in isolation. Teamwork and collaboration amplify individual efforts. Lieberman's experience building his company, Morning Brew, demonstrates how surrounding yourself with gritty, determined individuals can build resilience and perseverance. He stresses that the energy and attitudes of those around you are contagious.[2]

When I reflect on my own experiences, the role of grit stands out. During my time at IMG Academy, one of the most prestigious sports high schools in the U.S., I was constantly surrounded by athletes who were taller, stronger, faster, and more experienced than I was. At first, it was slightly intimidating. But over time I realized that I could take bits and pieces from each of them—their discipline, work ethic, and mindset—to improve myself. They taught me the importance of persistence and grit, not just in sports, but in every aspect of life. Watching my peers, dedication to their sports inspired me to push harder and adopt the mindset that, no matter how tough things get, quitting is never an option.

Lieberman's emphasis on diversity of thought also resonates. At IMG, I interacted with peers from all over the world, each bringing unique perspectives and cultural influences. This diversity expanded my vision and helped me understand problems from angles I hadn't considered before. Similarly, in Rome, I've been fortunate to build connections with people who think differently than I do. While it's not always comfortable to engage with those who challenge your views, this discomfort is where growth happens. It sharpens your creativity and develop innovation, enabling you to solve problems more effectively.

Whether it's through direct mentorship, collaboration, or observing talented individuals, surrounding yourself with people who excel in areas where you lack expertise accelerates your growth. At IMG, I learned not just from my coaches but also from my teammates, who excelled in their respective sports. In Rome, I've continued this practice by seeking out individuals who push me intellectually and physically. For those who don't have direct access to mentors or experts, podcasts, books, and videos can provide invaluable insights. For me, online mentors like Patrick Bet-David, Jordan Peterson, and Alex Hormozi have played a significant role in shaping my mindset. Their content serves as a constant reminder to think bigger, stay disciplined, and keep moving forward.

At the core of all this is the idea that the people around you shape your trajectory. Surrounding yourself with gritty, skilled, and diverse individuals creates an environment that fosters resilience, innovation, and a shared focus on growth. Reflecting on my journey, I'm grateful for the network of individuals—both in person and through digital platforms—who have challenged and inspired me.

To build the right team, consider these steps:

1. **Audit Your Circle:** Evaluate the people you spend the most time with. Are they uplifting and inspiring, or do they hold you back?
2. **Seek Diversity:** Engage with individuals who think differently and bring unique perspectives.
3. **Embrace Discomfort:** Growth happens outside your comfort zone. Surround yourself with people who challenge you to be better.
4. **Learn from the Best:** Identify individuals who excel in areas you want to improve and learn from their expertise.
5. **Leverage Media:** If direct access isn't possible, consume content from thought leaders who inspire you.

By consciously curating your circle, you can shorten your path to success, expand your vision, and unlock your full potential.

Unlike many teens and young adults who spend their adolescence growing up with the same friends, I did not have that luxury. However, I view it as a blessing. Because I never spent more than three years at any one school or in any one city, I was forced to adapt to eight different schools in eight different cities. Reflecting on it now, I am very thankful for the experience of building new "teams" and experiencing so many different cultures and ideologies without younger me really even noticing the differences.

Building the right team around you is crucial for several compelling reasons. Firstly, a well-assembled team of competent and motivated individuals can work more efficiently, leading to higher productivity and better use of resources. This efficiency stems from each member bringing their unique strengths to the table, allowing tasks to be completed swiftly and effectively. For example, Elon Musk's success is often attributed to the talented individuals he collaborated with, such as the group known as the "PayPal Mafia." The Fortune article "The PayPal Mafia still rules Silicon Valley" highlights how the PayPal alumni network shaped the tech industry. After PayPal was acquired by eBay for $1.5 billion, members like Peter Thiel, Reid Hoffman, and YouTube cofounders used their collective knowledge, resources, and influence to launch ventures such as LinkedIn, SpaceX, and Yelp. This example highlights the importance of surrounding yourself with people who challenge and elevate your thinking. Perspective, shaped by the company you keep, is key to success. Isolating yourself with only your own ideas or staying around average thinkers limits what you can achieve. Being with high-level thinkers not only expands your vision, but also sharpens your capabilities, leading to greater success.[3]

> "Energy is contagious; either you affect people or you infect people." —T. Harv Eker

A diverse team brings a variety of perspectives, skills, and experiences, igniting innovative solutions and better decision-making. This diversity is invaluable as it prevents groupthink and encourages creative problem-solving. When team members feel their unique contributions are valued, it leads to more engagement and investment in the team's success. A shared vision and common goals are the backbone of a successful team. When everyone is aligned, it creates a sense of unity and purpose that drives the team forward. This alignment not only makes it easier to achieve common objectives, but also boosts morale and job satisfaction. A positive and collaborative team environment reduces turnover and increases employee loyalty, creating a stable and committed workforce.

Effective problem-solving is another critical benefit of building the right team. With a well-balanced mix of skills and perspectives, challenges are tackled more efficiently and solutions are found more quickly. This problem-solving prowess is further enhanced by strong communication and collaboration within the team. When information flows smoothly, misunderstandings are minimized, and collaborative efforts are maximized, leading to higher quality work. Moreover, a strong team is characterized by its ability to complement each other's strengths, producing superior results. Each member can focus on what they do best, knowing that their colleagues will cover other areas. This synergy leads to a higher quality of work, as every aspect of a project benefits from the expertise of those best suited to handle it.

If you surround yourself with average people, you're bound to hear only average thoughts and opinions. These individuals won't speak the language of winners; instead, they'll share what they believe is possible, limited by the constraints they've imposed on themselves. In contrast, those who grind in silence, maintaining focus while the world is quiet, build a discipline that pushes them forward long after others have given up. It's a matter of perspective: where some see obstacles, winners see opportunities. Winners adopt a mindset that transcends the limits others set for them. By staying on mission, fighting through adversity, and sharpening your perspective, you unlock the key to winning in life. It's about pushing past mediocrity and constantly striving for greatness, no matter the environment you find yourself in.

Building a great team also contributes to leadership development within an organization. Identifying and nurturing future leaders from within the team ensures a steady pipeline of talent ready to take on more responsibilities. This development not only benefits the individuals but also strengthens the organization as a whole. Ultimately, the right team contributes significantly to the long-term success and sustainability of an organization. By consistently driving performance and achieving strategic goals, a strong team lays the foundation for ongoing success. Investing in building and maintaining the right team is an investment in the future, ensuring that the organization remains competitive and resilient in a constantly evolving landscape.

17
Anchored in Faith
Living in God's Timing

Faith, at its core, is more than just belief in God's existence. It is a mindset, a commitment, a perspective shift that enables us to see beyond our circumstances and trust in the unseen. When we are grounded in faith, we are not shaken by life's unpredictable twists and turns, because we know that God's plan is greater than what we can see. Faith teaches us to be so confident in God's plan that we no longer get upset when things don't go our way. Jeremiah 29:11 reminds us of this divine assurance: "'For I know the plans I have for you,' declares the Lord, 'plans to prosper you and not to harm you, plans to give you hope and a future'"(NIV). Even when life doesn't align with our expectations, we can trust that God's plan is unfolding perfectly, beyond what we can see in the moment. Faith gives us the ability to release our need for control and instead embrace the certainty that God's purpose for our lives is one of prosperity and hope, even if the path is not always clear. It is this trust that brings peace, allowing us to navigate the twists and turns of life with confidence that God is always at work, shaping our future according to His perfect will.

The beauty of God's creation reminds us of how deeply personal His design is. It's incredible to realize that the same God who created the mountains and oceans looked at each of us and decided that the world needed one of us too. This perspective reveals the intentionality behind our existence, showing that we are not here by accident but by divine purpose, crafted uniquely by the Creator of all things. This foundational belief in God's sovereignty gives us peace. It allows us to live with the assurance that no matter what happens, we are part of His intricate and perfect plan. When our faith in God is strong, our perspective shifts from worry to trust, from confusion to clarity, and from fear to hope.

Faith is not just a tool for hope; it is a lens through which we view the world. It transforms how we interpret our experiences, how we respond to challenges, and how we grow through adversity. With faith, we don't just see what's in front of us; we trust in what's behind the scenes. When we pray for amazing things, we must also recognize that challenges often come alongside them. There is always an opposing force at work, and if we're willing to face it, the outcome can be profoundly rewarding. Faith doesn't mean avoiding struggles; rather, it means trusting that, within those struggles, something greater is at work. When we ask for blessings, we should also be prepared for the difficulties that may accompany them, knowing that these challenges are part of God's refining process, leading us toward a higher purpose.

Maybe God ruined your plans so your plan wouldn't ruin you.

Comedian and podcaster George Janko uses the bird and the snake metaphor to illustrate how easily we can lose focus and fall into harmful patterns. In the story, a bird is placed in a cage with a snake. At first, the bird is terrified, flapping its wings and frantically trying to escape the danger. But over time, something changes. The bird gradually becomes more comfortable in the snake's presence, watching it closely and eventually drawing near. Finally, the bird, having lost all sense of the danger, hops into the snake's mouth and is consumed.[1]

This story serves as a warning: Just like the bird, we can become desensitized to the dangers around us if we aren't careful about where we direct our attention. At first, we might recognize the threats—sin, distractions, and negativity—but over time, if we allow ourselves to grow comfortable with them, we may become blind to the harm they can cause. These dangers don't usually strike all at once; rather, they creep in slowly, taking advantage of our inattention or complacency. Faith sharpens our awareness and helps us stay focused on what truly matters. It reminds us to keep our eyes fixed on what is life-giving and true, rather than allowing ourselves to drift toward what is destructive. With faith, we can guard against the subtle influences that might derail our spiritual journey and keep us from fulfilling God's purpose in our lives.

Faith enables us to see beyond our immediate circumstances. When we're at our lowest point, the only way forward is upward. Faith compels us to look up, knowing that even in the darkest moments, God is there, ready to lift us up. Our relationship with God can be likened to a captain and a crew member: We do the rowing, but God does the steering. *Faith teaches us to trust in God's guidance while still putting in our own effort. It is not passive. It is an active partnership where we do the work, but trust that God is directing us toward the right path.*

While God has given us everything we need to live justly, we still inflict harm on each other. Faith doesn't absolve us from responsibility; instead, it forces us to examine our actions and perspectives. We are responsible for how we treat others and how we navigate the challenges of life. Faith calls us to be part of the solution, recognizing that the way we live and respond to the world around us reflects our deeper beliefs.

The process of cultivating faith is ongoing. It's a daily commitment to seeing life through a divine lens, knowing that what we experience on the surface is only a small part of the bigger picture. When we operate from a place of faith, we understand that the challenges, the setbacks, and even the moments of suffering are all part of God's plan to shape us, refine us, and guide us toward our destiny. Faith transforms our mindset. It moves us from a reactionary way of living—where we respond to what's happening around us—to a proactive and trust-filled life where we are anchored in the belief that God is always working, even when we don't see it. *Faith helps us interpret life not by what happens to us but by what God is doing through us.*

The Role of Others in Shaping Our Perspective

Faith not only shapes our own perspective but is profoundly influenced by the people we allow into our lives. Proverbs 27:17 reminds us, "As iron sharpens iron, so one person sharpens another"(NIV). This means that while faith is deeply personal, it is also communal. The people we surround ourselves with can either dull or sharpen our perspectives, making it essential to choose our relationships wisely.

We do not rise to the level of our dreams, but to the level of those around us. Our growth, our ability to develop a godly perspective, and our capacity to rise through challenges are often determined by the people who walk alongside us. Some people in our lives, though well-meaning, may not be equipped to handle the toughest moments. Like butter knives trying to cut through something they aren't designed for, they might not have what it takes to help us grow. If we're not intentional about the connections we keep, we may find ourselves surrounded by people who aren't capable of sharpening us in meaningful ways. Faith is not just about passive belief—it's about action, and sometimes that action means reevaluating the people we keep close. Ask yourself: "Do the people in my life have the ability to heal me after they've cut me with their words?" True friends, like doctors, don't shy away from hard conversations. They cut, but they heal. They challenge us, helping us see beyond our pain. These are the kinds of people that strengthen our faith and sharpen our perspective.

The story in Matthew 9 serves as a powerful reminder of the impact others can have on our faith journey. Jesus heals a paralyzed man, not because of the man's own faith, but because of the faith of his friends. This shows that our faith journey is not a solo endeavor. The people we choose to align ourselves with can have a profound impact on our spiritual growth. The right people lift us up, hold us accountable, and even carry us when we are too weak to carry ourselves. Surrounding ourselves with those who sharpen us, rather than dull us, is essential for spiritual growth and the development of a strong, faith-filled perspective.

A profound story illustrates how our understanding of God is shaped by our proximity to Him. In the story, a young boy asks his father how big God is. The father points to an airplane in the sky and asks the boy how large it appears. From a distance, the airplane looks tiny, almost insignificant. The boy responds that the airplane seems very small. The father later takes the boy to an airport to see an airplane up close. Standing next to the massive aircraft, the boy is amazed, marveling at how enormous it is. The father explains that God is like this airplane—His presence and impact in our lives grow as we draw closer to Him.[2]

This story shows that the closer we draw to God, the larger and more powerful He becomes in our lives. When we are distant or disconnected, God can feel small and far off. But as we deepen our relationship with Him, we experience His presence more fully. The people we surround ourselves with also influence this closeness. Faith-filled friends can help us draw nearer to God, making His presence loom larger, while superficial connections can leave us feeling distant from Him. This highlights the importance of choosing relationships that bring us closer to God and His influence in our lives.

In essence, the people we allow into our inner circle play a vital role in shaping our faith. They influence how we see God, how we see ourselves, and how we navigate life's challenges. If we want to grow in faith, wisdom, and perspective, we need to intentionally surround ourselves with people who sharpen us—those who challenge our thinking, strengthen our belief, and help us draw closer to God.

Faith and Patience: Seeing the Bigger Picture

Faith and patience are deeply connected because, while we often crave immediate answers and quick solutions, faith teaches us to trust in God's perfect timing. Gospel singer Kirk Franklin uses a vivid analogy to explain this: Microwavable meals might be fast, but they aren't always fully cooked or satisfying. In contrast, Grandma's Sunday dinner—prepared with care, marinated overnight, and slowly cooked—is far more rewarding. This analogy reminds us that the things God is working on in our lives, much like Grandma's carefully prepared meal, take time. They aren't rushed or thrown together; they are being refined and perfected according to His plan.[3]

Just as the flavor of Grandma's meal is enhanced by the time and attention it receives, so the outcomes of our lives are enriched by the waiting process. Faith gives us the ability to trust that, even when we can't see the results right away, something far greater is being prepared for us. It allows us to endure the waiting period, knowing that what God is crafting is more fulfilling and meaningful than anything we could rush into existence on our own. By embracing patience, we allow God to marinate the plans for our lives, ensuring they reach their full potential and purpose in His perfect time.

God's timing requires patience, and patience requires faith. The story of Joseph in the Bible serves as a powerful example of this. Joseph had a vision of his destiny, but before that vision could become a reality, he had to endure years of hardship, betrayal, and waiting. He saw the end goal—ruling and feeding his brothers—but he didn't foresee the journey he would have to take. Had Joseph known about the pit and the prison, he might have been tempted to give up. Yet those difficult experiences were not setbacks; they were essential parts of God's preparation process, refining Joseph for the throne.

This principle applies to our lives today. God often gives us a glimpse of our destiny without revealing the full path. The journey, with its waiting, struggles, and detours, is necessary for preparing us for the future He has in store. If we were shown the entire journey ahead, we might become discouraged, but faith helps us trust that every step, even the hardest ones, is moving us toward something far greater than we can imagine. Each challenge serves a purpose in shaping us for the fulfillment of God's plan.

"God will never remove something from our lives without replacing it with something better." —Billy Graham

Life often teaches us lessons in one of two ways: the hard way or the harder way. Those lessons tend to come through the most challenging experiences. While God, in His grace, provides us with opportunities to learn the easy way, we often ignore the subtle signs. George Janko reflects on how we sometimes overlook these chances, thinking we've avoided the consequences, only to be hit with a harsher lesson later. It's worth asking ourselves: What's the most difficult lesson we've learned recently, and how many times were we given the chance to learn it differently? Discipline, while uncomfortable, is not meant to harm us. Rather, it is God's way of showing love, guiding us to grow and align with His purpose.[4] God teaches through discipline, not to harm us, but because He loves us and wants us to grow.

Janko recalls a powerful analogy, saying that in school, you learn first and then take the test. But with God, you're often given the test first, and then you learn. Life is held in God's hands, not the devil's, and even the forces we perceive as powerful—whether trials, demons, or the world around us—only move when God allows it. Janko shares a personal story, reflecting on his fear when he first entered the entertainment industry. His mom reassured him with a profound truth: "If God says 'action,' who has the authority to say 'cut'?"[5] Only God. This perspective gave him the confidence to trust in God's control over every situation.

Faith Transforms Struggles into Strengths

Faith has the power to take our struggles and turn them into strengths. Through faith, we find meaning in hardship, and we begin to understand that every challenge is an opportunity for growth. It's not about avoiding difficulties but about allowing faith to shape us through them, transforming pain into purpose.

The transformation through faith is beautifully captured in a poem by rapper and lyricist Cassidy, who writes, "When you walk with God, no strength is lost so keep walking. When you talk with God, no breath is lost so keep talking."[6] His words remind us that walking in faith doesn't deplete us — it renews us. Even in moments of waiting or uncertainty, faith gives meaning to the journey. Struggles aren't wasted; they're repurposed into strength when God is at the center.

This reflection speaks to the enduring power of faith, especially in times of struggle. With God as our guide, even the hardest moments become part of a greater design. Faith shifts our perspective — from fear to trust, from loss to preparation. Struggles, doubts, and challenges are not detours; they're the very tools God uses to build our resilience, shape our purpose, and prepare us for what's next..

Often, we fall in love with the blessing and forget about the One who gave it to us. We can become so enamored with the blessings we receive that we polish them, elevate them, and put them on a pedestal, all the while neglecting our relationship with the Blesser—God Himself. In our pursuit of what we think we want or need, we can lose sight of the true source of our strength and fulfillment, which is our connection with God. When we rely too heavily on the material or worldly blessings in our lives, we risk turning them into idols. These blessings, if detached from the Giver, can break us, leaving us feeling empty and in despair.

God sometimes uses the blessings He gives us as a way to test where our true devotion lies. When we encounter struggles, our instinct might be to question why, focusing on the challenges rather than what they are teaching us. The blessing itself can't heal or fix us—only God, the Blesser, can do that. Our true strength doesn't come from the material things we accumulate or the successes we achieve, but from maintaining a strong, connected relationship with the One who provides those blessings in the first place. Faith helps us shift our focus back to God, reminding us to put Him first, especially during difficult times.

This shift in perspective, from relying on blessings to relying on God, is key to navigating struggles with faith. Rather than asking, "Why?" when challenges arise, we can look back and see how God has worked in our lives. By reflecting on who helped us, what healed us, and how we grew through our difficulties, we begin to appreciate the journey. Instead of seeking answers to why things happen, faith allows us to trust in God's process, recognizing that each trial brings growth and prepares us for something greater. With this mindset, we can g ive thanks for both the challenges and the blessings, knowing that God's guidance is always at work in our lives.

Faith and Self-Denial: Choosing a Higher Perspective

Faith often calls us to resist what is easy, comfortable, or immediately gratifying in order to embrace a higher perspective. Practicing self-discipline is a spiritual exercise that leads us closer to God, and through it we learn to align our desires with His will. This means choosing to prioritize what is spiritually nourishing over temporary distractions and indulgences.

One reflection on this discipline speaks to the need to turn toward God instead of mindlessly scrolling through social media or engaging in other distractions. The Bible frequently emphasizes self-discipline, reminding us to choose what is better over what is easy. It's fine to engage in light entertainment, but faith invites us to pursue something deeper—something that will enrich our souls rather than simply pass the time. When we pray and have personal conversations with God, we're not just following a routine; we're building and nurturing a relationship with the Creator of the universe. This understanding transforms prayer into something profoundly intimate—a moment where we engage directly with the One who knows us best and loves us unconditionally.

Each time we set aside distractions and choose to speak with God, we deepen that relationship. We're not just speaking to a distant figure, but to a personal God who desires to guide and connect with us. This realization—that we are nurturing a real, personal relationship with God—makes every moment of communication with Him incredibly significant. Choosing to spend time in conversation with God rather than focusing on worldly distractions shifts our perspective and brings us closer to His presence.

Steve Harvey emphasizes the transformative power of writing down your dreams and aligning them with faith in God's promises. In his speech, he advises creating a detailed list of everything you want, referencing the scripture in Habakkuk 2:2: "Write down the revelation and make it plain on tablets so that a herald may run with it" (NIV). In other words, write the vision and make it plain—then revisit it daily with faith and expectation. By taking this step, Harvey explains, you signal to God that you believe in His ability to bring your vision to fruition. Extending this idea, it's important to protect your dreams from those who may project doubts or limitations, as staying true to God's vision requires unwavering faith, even in the face of external negativity. Trusting in God means holding firm to the dreams He has placed in your heart and believing they can be achieved through disciplined action and prayer.[7]

The blessings we pray for often come with challenges. Instead of asking for an easy life, people of faith ask for the strength to handle the blessings and responsibilities God gives them. *Sometimes, the real challenge isn't receiving the blessing, but managing the responsibility and weight that comes with it.* Faith, in this sense, involves understanding that sacrifice, discipline, and perseverance are necessary to carry the blessings God provides. It's not about avoiding difficulty, but about learning to embrace the challenges that help us grow.

In a world filled with distractions and shortcuts, faith encourages us to rise above and choose what aligns with God's purpose. Self-discipline is not about deprivation; it's about gaining something far greater. It's about making decisions that draw us closer to God's plan and deepen our faith journey. When we choose faith over convenience, discipline over indulgence, and God's vision over worldly success, we develop a higher perspective—one that views life through the lens of eternity. Faith isn't about seeking quick rewards; it's about long-term fulfillment and aligning ourselves with God's perfect will.

> *"When you get what you want that is God's direction.*
> *When you don't get what you want that is God's protection."*
> —*Shannon L. Alder*

Faith and Trust in God's Plan

Faith is a journey of trusting in God's plan, even when we don't understand it. Life presents us with challenges, opportunities, and moments that force us to question our path. But through faith we learn to trust that God's plan is greater than anything we could imagine, and that even when things seem difficult, He is always in control. Our faith becomes real when we reach the end of our own strength and realize we can't handle life on our own. In these moments, God shows His power and reminds us to put Him first in everything we do.

Another perspective highlights that God gives us opportunities, but it's our responsibility to act on them. Faith isn't passive; when God provides us with blessings or opportunities, He's giving us the raw materials to work with—like a tree. It's up to us to see the potential in those materials, to envision what they could become. Whether it's a table, a chair, or something else entirely, faith requires us to co-create with God, taking the opportunities He provides and turning them into something meaningful. This means we need to act, trusting in the potential God has placed in front of us.

Leonardo da Vinci referenced that everything God offers comes at the price of labor. This reinforces the idea that faith isn't about waiting passively for blessings to fall into our laps; it's about working for them. While God provides the guidance and the resources, we must be willing to put in the effort. Faith requires perseverance and action, trusting that as we work, God is leading us toward the fulfillment of His promises. The Bible offers countless insights into trusting God's plan, and while every book contains wisdom, here are a few of my favorites that provide a strong foundation for understanding faith, guidance, and God's promises. Each of these books offers unique lessons that illuminate different aspects of our faith journey.

John: Tells the story of Jesus' life, the ultimate example of trust in God's plan.

Romans: Lays out basic Christian beliefs, grounding us in faith.

Ephesians: Teaches us how to live a holy life, guided by faith and trust.

Philippians: Explores the joy and trials of life, showing us how to trust God in all circumstances.

Psalms: A collection of praise, prayer, faith, emotion, and worship, demonstrating the importance of trusting God through highs and lows.

Proverbs: Offers wisdom for living wisely, reminding us that trust in God is foundational to making good decisions.

Genesis: The story of creation and God's covenant with humanity, a testament to His enduring plan.

Exodus: The Israelites' deliverance from Egypt and God's guidance, showing how faith leads to freedom.

Acts: The growth of the early Church after Jesus' resurrection, illustrating the power of faith in action.

Hebrews: Presents Jesus as the ultimate high priest and mediator, affirming our trust in His work on our behalf.

James: Practical advice for living out faith through actions, emphasizing the need to combine trust with work.

Revelation: A prophetic vision of the end times and God's ultimate triumph, reminding us that God's plan is victorious in the end.

Together, these books offer a solid foundation for understanding and trusting God's plan, reminding us that faith is not just about belief, but also about taking action.

The Full Picture of Faith and Perspective

It's clear that faith is not only a personal journey but also a communal one. Faith shapes how we see the world, ourselves, and our future. It transforms our perspective on everything from struggle to success, helping us find peace in the midst of uncertainty.

King Solomon shares a beautiful reflection in Ecclesiastes about being at peace with oneself, learning to accept life as it comes, and still trusting that God is sovereign. This is the essence of faith—finding peace in the struggle, knowing that God is in control. As Solomon writes in Ecclesiastes 3:11 (NIV), "He has made everything beautiful in its time." In other words, God works on His own timeline—reminding us that we don't need to have all the answers or be perfect right now. Faith is about walking through life with the assurance that God is guiding us, even when we can't see the full picture.

This assurance of God's guidance leads to another profound truth: God is always near, gently knocking at the door, ready to bring order to our chaos. However, while God patiently waits for us to open the door, Satan sneaks in through the window, bringing disorder and distraction. Faith requires an active choice—not just to let God in, but to trust Him to guide us and protect our lives from chaos. True faith is not passive; it calls us to embrace God's presence intentionally, finding peace and perspective amid life's struggles.

We must stop chasing after things and start manifesting what God has already placed within us. Chasing after dreams or material success can often lead us in circles, never leaving us truly satisfied. Instead, faith calls us to trust in a higher source, to manifest what God has already designed for us. Faith isn't passive; it's active. It requires prayer, connection with God, and trust that He will guide us toward what's meant for us. God should mean everything to us. When God becomes everything, our perspective changes. We no longer live for ourselves but for something greater, trusting that every moment, every challenge, and every joy is part of God's plan. In that trust, we find peace, purpose, and perspective.

Faith is the lens through which we view the world, transforming every aspect of our lives. Whether it's the struggles that shape us, the relationships that sharpen us, or the trust that sustains us, faith is the foundation for everything. King Solomon's reflection about accepting life as it comes while trusting that God is sovereign captures the ultimate goal of faith: to walk through life with trust, knowing that we are held by the One who created us, guides us, and has a plan for our lives.

Faith is not just about belief; it's about perspective. It changes how we see our circumstances, how we handle challenges, and how we approach the future. When we put our faith in God, we are not walking alone. We walk with the assurance that He is steering the ship, working all things for our good, and preparing us for something greater than we could ever imagine.

Wisdom from the Highest Source

As we've explored throughout this book, faith shapes our perspective, strengthens us in our struggles, and directs us toward a deeper relationship with God. But no source of wisdom is greater than that which comes directly from God's Word. The book of Proverbs, my favorite book in the Bible, is known for its timeless insights and offers powerful reminders about living a life rooted in faith, wisdom, and purpose. Let these words be a source of strength and reflection as you continue your own journey of faith and growth.

1. **Proverbs 3:13** – "Happy are those who find wisdom, and those who get understanding."

2. **Proverbs 13:8** – "Wealth is a ransom for a person's life, but the poor get no threats."

3. **Proverbs 16:3** – "Commit your work to the Lord, and your plans will be established."

4. **Proverbs 16:9** – "The human mind plans the way, but the Lord directs the steps."

5. **Proverbs 18:15** – "The mind of the intelligent acquires knowledge, and the ear of the wise seeks knowledge."

6. **Proverbs 19:8** – "To get wisdom is to love oneself; to keep understanding is to prosper."

7. **Proverbs 26:4** – "Do not answer fools according to their folly, or you will be a fool yourself."

8. **Proverbs 27:1** – "Do not boast about tomorrow, for you do not know what a day may bring."

9. **Proverbs 27:2** – "Let another praise you, and not your own mouth—a stranger, and not your own lips."

10. **Proverbs 27:6** – "Well meant are the wounds a friend inflicts, but profuse are the kisses of an enemy."

11. **Proverbs 27:19** – "Just as water reflects the face, so one human heart reflects another."

12. **Proverbs 27:23-24** – "Know well the condition of your flocks, and give attention to your herds; for riches do not last forever, nor a crown for all generations."

13. **Proverbs 28:18** – "One who walks in integrity will be safe, but whoever follows crooked ways will fall into the pit."

14. **Proverbs 28:26** – "Those who trust in their own wits are fools, but those who walk in wisdom come through safely."

15. **Proverbs 28:27** – "Whoever gives to the poor will lack nothing, but one who turns a blind eye will get many curses."

16. **Proverbs 29:3** – "A child who loves wisdom makes a parent glad."

17. **Proverbs 29:11** – "Fools give full vent to their anger, but the wise quietly hold it back."

18. **Proverbs 29:17** – "Discipline your children, and they will give you rest; they will give delight to your heart."

19. **Proverbs 30:5** – "Every word of God proves true; He is a shield to those who take refuge in Him."

20. **Proverbs 31:3** – "Do not give your strength to women, your ways to those who destroy kings."

21. **Proverbs 31:8** – "Speak out for those who cannot speak, for the rights of all the destitute."

22. **Proverbs 31:10** – "A capable wife who can find? She is far more precious than jewels."

18

Endings as Beginnings
One Step at a Time

Imagine planting a seed and understanding that while it's covered, it's actually being protected. We often crave validation and want others to see our progress, leading us to prematurely uncover the seed. However, just like in nature, growth requires patience and unseen nurturing. If you went outside and unearthed your seed daily for others to see, it would never grow. The seed needs time beneath the soil, absorbing nutrients and water away from prying eyes. This period of being unseen is crucial for its development.

We must be comfortable with tending to our dreams and goals privately, pouring effort and care into them when no one else can see. In time, the seed will break through the ground, visible to all. At that moment, you won't need to seek validation. Your growth will be evident, whether others wish to acknowledge it or not. Patience is essential in this process. It helps us build a stronger, more resilient perspective, understanding that the most significant growth often happens out of sight. Trust in the process, and, in due time, your efforts will flourish unmistakably.

This book represents the culmination of years of exploration, reflection, and growth. It began as a personal journal; a space to capture the lessons life has taught me, and it evolved into a guide I hope will inspire you to navigate your own journey with clarity, resilience, and purpose. What started as an idea at age nineteen and came to fruition at age twenty-one is more than a collection of insights—it is a testament to the transformative power of patience and perspective and the value of embracing life as a process that unfolds over time. None of the lessons or transformations presented in this book occurred instantly; they took time, effort, and intentionality. Growth is not a sprint but a journey—a series of small steps that, over time, lead to profound change. Patience is the thread that ties together all these lessons, reminding us to trust the process and embrace the work required to become the person we are meant to be.

As you learn to trust your compass within, I hope this book has confirmed some of the benefits of listening to this divine instrument seeded by God.

- **Clarity in Decision-Making**: Trusting the compass within helps you find direction amidst uncertainty.
- **Authenticity**: The compass within guides you to live a life true to your values and passions.
- **Increased Confidence**: Relying on your inner compass builds self-trust and assurance.

- **Reduced Regret:** Decisions made with the compass within often feel more intentional and satisfying.
- **Peace of Mind:** Following the compass within brings a sense of calm and alignment.
- **Greater Resilience:** Your compass within provides steady guidance in times of challenge and change.
- **Improved Focus:** It helps quiet distractions and keeps you aligned with your priorities.
- **Stronger Boundaries:** The compass within shows you when to say yes or no to protect your energy.
- **Deeper Self-Awareness:** Listening to the compass within reveals insights about your true desires.
- **Enhanced Creativity:** The compass within often sparks innovative and inspired ideas.
- **Aligned Opportunities:** You attract circumstances that resonate with the direction your compass points.
- **Less Need for Validation:** Trusting the compass within diminishes dependence on external approval.
- **Better Relationships:** The compass within guides you toward genuine and meaningful connections.
- **Stress Reduction:** It helps release the anxiety caused by chasing others' expectations.
- **Life Satisfaction:** Living by the compass within leads to a more fulfilling and purposeful life.
- **Personal Growth:** The compass within encourages learning and evolution on your unique journey.
- **Spiritual Connection:** Following the compass within fosters a deeper connection to your soul or higher self.
- **Quick Adaptability:** The compass within helps you navigate life's twists with grace.
- **Increased Joy:** Living in alignment with your compass within brings true happiness.
- **Empowerment:** The compass within strengthens your ability to lead your life with intention.

Life is a journey shaped by patience, perspective, and perseverance. Every lesson, every challenge, and every triumph along the way is part of a grander process of growth. This book has explored the many facets of that journey, from understanding the power of perspective to embracing individuality, building discipline, and learning to trust in faith. But at the heart of all these principles lies patience—the quiet force that holds everything together and allows true transformation to take place.

Patience teaches us that growth takes time. Whether it's reframing how we see the world, climbing the metaphorical mountains of life, or paying the price for success, nothing meaningful happens overnight. Perspective, for example, requires time to develop. *Perspective is not just a sudden shift but a gradual process of unlearning old habits, challenging limiting beliefs, and seeing possibilities where others see problems.* Similarly, climbing any mountain—literal or figurative—demands preparation, resilience, and the understanding that the climb itself shapes us more than the summit ever could.

Success, too, is a slow burn. It comes at a price, often requiring sacrifices and delayed gratification. Patience is what allows us to endure the discomfort, stay focused, and trust that consistent effort will eventually bear fruit. This principle extends to the mental battles we fight daily. The "War Room" within us demands persistence and resolve. Patience reminds us that lasting victories are achieved over time, through consistent effort, even when progress feels imperceptible.

Taking action is the bridge between dreams and reality, but progress often feels frustratingly slow. Here, patience teaches us to trust the process, celebrate small wins, and understand that each step forward compounds over time. Visualization, too, is a testament to patience. Holding a clear picture of our goals is powerful, but bringing them to life requires effort and the willingness to embrace the waiting period. The clearer our vision and the more patient we are, the closer we move toward our dreams.

Living authentically—standing firm in our individuality—is another practice that takes time. Patience is essential as we discover who we truly are, peel back societal expectations, and find the courage to embrace our unique selves. It's a journey of peeling back layers, one by one, until we reach a place of authenticity. Along the way, patience reminds us that the rewards of individuality far outweigh the temporary discomfort of not fitting in.

Patience also plays a vital role in learning. True growth doesn't come from rushing but from engaging with challenges and failures, trusting that every new insight and skill will serve us in the future. Whether we're cultivating a love of learning, building discipline, or surrounding ourselves with the right team, patience helps us see that meaningful relationships, habits, and skills take time to develop. Trust isn't built overnight, and collaboration requires consistent effort. The right people will come into our lives at the right time, and, with patience, we can cultivate connections that sharpen and inspire us.

Faith, perhaps the ultimate expression of patience, teaches us to trust in what we cannot see. It calls us to surrender control and believe that every step is part of a greater plan, even when the path ahead is unclear. Just as a seed must remain buried before it grows, so our dreams often require time to manifest. Patience teaches us to nurture what matters, even when results are not immediate, and to trust that the waiting period is not wasted, but is a time of unseen growth.

Finally, patience ties all these principles together. It's the thread that weaves through the entire journey, reminding us to trust the process, endure the struggles, and wait for the right time for our efforts to bear fruit. Whether it's learning from losses, embracing individuality, or finding faith in the unseen, patience ensures we stay the course and remain committed to becoming the best version of ourselves.

In a world that often glorifies speed and instant gratification, patience invites us to slow down and appreciate the journey. It reminds us that true transformation doesn't happen overnight, but is the result of consistent effort, trust, and resilience. Good things come to those who wait—not passively, but with active engagement and unwavering belief in the process. As you move forward in your own journey, may patience guide you, perspective inspire you, and the lessons within these pages empower you to embrace life's challenges with strength and clarity.

This is not just the conclusion of a book. It is an invitation to continue your own journey. Life's greatest transformations rarely happen overnight, but with patience, resilience, and the right mindset, they are always within reach. Embrace the lessons, celebrate the progress, and trust in the unfolding of your journey.

The path ahead is yours to create, one step at a time.

Notes

CHAPTER 1

1. Dyer, Wayne. "When You Change the Way You Look at Things, the Things You Look at Change." Medium, 4.7 years ago, https://medium.com/@ankushskapoor/when-you-change-the-way-you-look-at-things-the-things-you-look-at-change-dr-wayne-dyer-f49dc2b65191.
2. Plato. *The Republic.* Translated by Benjamin Jowett, Dover Publications, 2000.
3. Plato. *The Apology.* Translated by Benjamin Jowett, Dover Publications, 2009.
4. Hall, Manly P. *The Initiates of the Flame.* Philosophical Research Society, 1922.
5. Milan. "Luke Belmar Reveals the Power of the Mind." *YouTube,* 20 Jan. 2025, www.youtube.com/watch?v=09HJKepCY8E.
6. Fay, Derik. "Derik Fay on Building Wealth Through Relationships." *YouTube,* 20 Jan. 2025, https://youtube.com/shorts/t2S_jvomq2o?si=VYqOLIK2hPIE6WVH.
7. Housel, Morgan. "Some Things I Think." *Collab Fund,* 26 Apr. 2023, https://collabfund.com/blog/thoughts/.
8. Swindoll, Charles R. Life Is 10% What Happens to You and 90% How You React. Worthy Publishing, 2024. Ebooks.com, https://www.ebooks.com/en-us/book/210591026/life-is-10-what-happens-to-you-and-90-how-you-react/charles-r-swindoll/.
9. Goleman, Daniel. *Emotional Intelligence: Why It Can Matter More Than IQ.* Bantam Books, 1995
10. Land, George, and Beth Jarman. *Breakpoint and Beyond: Mastering the Future Today.* HarperBusiness, 1992.
11. Von, Theo. "Jordan Peterson | This Past Weekend w/ Theo Von #460." *This Past Weekend,* 13 May 2023, https://www.youtube.com/watch?v=AhZLh_sApPo.
12. "Jim Rohn: Why Not You, Why Not Now." *YouTube,* uploaded by Brent Hosaka, 17 November 2014, https://www.youtube.com/watch?v=Q7bPssMKxYI.
13. The Roommates. "Should Men Today Get Married?" *YouTube,* 16 Feb. 2021, https://www.youtube.com/watch?v=kIxzBNqHtoA.

CHAPTER 2

1. Lao Tzu. "The Journey of a Thousand Miles Begins with One Step." Socratic Method Research, www.socratic-method.com/quote-meanings/lao-tzu-the-journey-of-a-thousand-miles-begins-with-one-step.
2. Hillary, Edmund. "It Is Not the Mountain We Conquer but Ourselves." Enliven the Mind, www.enliventhemind.com/motivational-quote-guides/edmund-hillary-quote-it-is-not-the-mountain-we-conquer-but-ourselves/.

CHAPTER 3

1. Tucker, Ian. "Ellen Hendriksen: 'We Are Each Our Own Worst Critic.'" *The Guardian,* 14 Apr. 2018, https://www.theguardian.com/science/2018/apr/14/ellen-hendriksen-we-are-each-our-own-worst-critic-social-anxiety-disorder-interview.
2. Jung, Carl. "I Am Not What Happened to Me. I Am What I Choose to Become." Quotes Guide. https://quotes.guide/carl-jung/quote/i-am-not-what-happened-to-me-i-am-what-i-choose-to-become/
3. World Golf Hall of Fame. "Tiger Woods: World Golf Hall of Fame Acceptance Speech (2022 Induction)." *YouTube,* 9 Mar. 2022, https://www.youtube.com/watch?v=ny8HK_FmU_g.
4. Aurelius, Marcus. "You Have Power over Your Mind – Not Outside Events. Realize This, and You Will Find Strength." Philosiblog, 25 Sept. 2013,

https://philosiblog.com/2013/09/25/
you-have-power-over-your-mind-not-
outside-events-realize-this-and-you-will-
find-strength/.

CHAPTER 4

1. Beck, Glenn, host. "Jocko Willink." *The Glenn Beck Podcast*, episode 38, Blaze Media, 25 May 2019, https://www.youtube.com/watch?v=h1ZOtFVup84.
2. Rogan, Joe, host. "Joe Rogan Experience #1080 - David Goggins." *The Joe Rogan Experience*, PowerfulJRE, 19 Feb. 2018, https://www.youtube.com/watch?v=5tSTk1083VY.
3. Bartlett, Steven. *Happy Sexy Millionaire: Unexpected Truths about Fulfillment, Love, and Success*. Yellow Kite, 2021
4. Williamson, Chris. "17 Raw Lessons About Human Nature - Steven Bartlett (4K)." *YouTube*, 2 Oct. 2023, https://www.youtube.com/watch?v=JBgwF8aHByI.
5. Keuilian, Bedros. "My $200,000,000 Morning Routine | The Bedros Keuilian Show E020." *YouTube*, 14 Feb. 2023, https://www.youtube.com/watch?v=lLhz4fulKko.
6. Ranjan, Nandjee. ""I Trained 4 Years to Run 9 Seconds": Shaquille O'Neal Shows Love to Usain Bolt's Incredible Mentality." The SportsRush, 13 Aug. 2023, https://thesportsrush.com/nba-news-i-trained-4-years-to-run-9-seconds-shaquille-oneal-shows-love-to-usain-bolts-incredible-mentality/.
7. Rohn, Jim. "Discipline is the bridge between goals and accomplishment." *Goodreads*, https://www.goodreads.com/quotes/28439-discipline-is-the-bridge-between-goals-and-accomplishment.
8. Shetty, Jay. "Kobe Bryant's Last Great Interview on How to Find Purpose in Life | Kobe Bryant & Jay Shetty." *Jay Shetty Podcast*, 19 Sep. 2020, https://www.youtube.com/watch?v=g2cQ2kD6lzs.
9. Shetty, Jay. "Kobe Bryant's Last Great Interview on How to Find Purpose in Life | Kobe Bryant & Jay Shetty." *Jay Shetty Podcast*, 19 Sep.

2020, https://www.youtube.com/watch?v=g2cQ2kD6lzs.

CHAPTER 5

1. TeamSoul. "20 Marie Forleo Quotes to Make You Aware of Your Highest Potential." Fearless Soul, 20 Feb. 2018, https://iamfearlesssoul.com/20-marie-forleo-quotes/.
2. Fallon, Jimmy, host. "Tim Grover on Training Kobe Bryant and Michael Jordan (Extended)." *The Tonight Show Starring Jimmy Fallon*, 27 Oct. 2023, https://www.youtube.com/watch?v=lxAAr-G8kRI.
3. Maxwell, John C. The 15 Invaluable Laws of Growth: Live Them and Reach Your Potential. Goodreads, https://www.goodreads.com/work/quotes/19086727-the-15-invaluable-laws-of-growth.
4. Roll, Rich, host. "Change Your Brain: Neuroscientist Dr. Andrew Huberman | Rich Roll Podcast." *YouTube*, 20 July 2020, https://www.youtube.com/watch?v=SwQhKFMxmDY.
5. Ghiorghiu, Sebastian, host. "Sebb X Luke Belmar: The Simple Truth." *YouTube*, 29 Nov. 2022, https://www.youtube.com/watch?v=nGV6DnQQ88M.
6. SnewJ Knows, host. "Meet the Ex-Con Who Makes $2 Million Per Month! ($30 Million Estate Tour) | Wes Watson." *YouTube*, 7 May 2023, https://www.youtube.com/watch?v=-iVZuv77ptQ&t=1s.
7. Abdelnour, Ziad K. "Don't Think Outside the Box. Think like There Is No Box." Goodreads, https://www.goodreads.com/quotes/711114-don-t-think-outside-the-box-think-like-there-is-no.

CHAPTER 6

8. Roy Baumeister and Mark Leary (1995), "The need to belong: Desire for interpersonal attachments as a fundamental human motivation," *Psychological Bulletin*, 117(3), 497–529. https://doi.org/10.1037/0033-2909.117.3.497.
9. Eisenberger, Naomi I., et al. "Does Rejection Hurt? An fMRI Study of

Social Exclusion." *Science*, vol. 302, no. 5643, 2003, pp. 290–292. *American Association for the Advancement of Science*, doi:10.1126/science.1089134.

10. Chou, Hui-Tzu Grace, and Nicholas Edge. "'They Are Happier and Having Better Lives than I Am': The Impact of Using Facebook on Perceptions of Others' Lives." *Cyberpsychology, Behavior, and Social Networking*, vol. 15, no. 2, Mary Ann Liebert, 9 Feb. 2012, https://doi.org/10.1089/cyber.2011.0324.

11. Interview, "Author Brene Brown on the Difference Between Belonging and Fitting In," September 12, 2017, CBS News, https://www.cbsnews.com/news/author-brene-brown-social-scientist-new-book-braving-the-wilderness/

12. Article, "Overcoming the Fear of Rejection," 2005, Denis Waitley's Weekly Ezine, https://www.ideaman.net/articles/sales/OvercomeFearofRejectionDW.pdf?utm

13. Video, "Doctor Gabor Mate: The Shocking Link Between Kindness & Illness!," The Diary of a CEO, 12 Oct. 2023, https://www.youtube.com/watch?v=L7zWT3l3DVo.

14. "Off-White Founder Virgil Abloh Interview on Education, Art, Culture, and Design." XQ America, 21 Sept. 2020, www.youtube.com/watch?v=hU39eXYMShA.

CHAPTER 7

1. "Jay Shetty: The 3 Simple Things A Happy Life Needs | E119." The Diary of a CEO, 14 Feb. 2022, www.youtube.com/watch?v=nYrjhv-AFZA&t=5410s.

2. "Eric Thomas | Motivational Speech | How Bad Do You." Nathan Scaglione, 22 July 2015, www.youtube.com/watch?v=6vuetQSwFW8.

3. "23 Harsh Truths Nobody Wants to Admit - Alex Hormozi (4K)." Chris Williamson, 21 Aug. 2023, www.youtube.com/watch?v=M4PzOjM5BJQ.

4. de Botton, Alain. "Loneliness Is a Tax You Have to Pay to Atone for a Certain Complexity of Mind." Goodreads, https://www.goodreads.com/quotes/11620836-loneliness-is-a-tax-you-have-to-pay-to-atone.

5. "Will Smith on What It Takes to Chase Your Dreams." Fry Sultani, 18 Jan. 2020, www.youtube.com/watch?v=1Jx6rWJ1zz8&t=3s.

6. "Monk Mode - Best Decision I've Ever Made." Paul Han, 20 Dec. 2023, www.youtube.com/watch?v=pteafDCotCM.

7. "NVIDIA CEO Jensen Huang Reveals Keys to AI, Leadership." Columbia Business School, 16 Oct. 2023, www.youtube.com/watch?v=MwiM_nPyx5Y.

8. Press Trust of India, "People Regret Not Chasing Dreams Over Unfulfilled Duties," Hindustan Times, May 30, 2018, https://www.hindustantimes.com/more-lifestyle/people-regret-not-chasing-dreams-over-unfulfilled-duties-says-study/story-qXBc8SKNrTIkIn8kRhdT3L.html.

9. Alan Lightman, "The Importance of Quiet Time," Daily Good, May 20, 2018, https://www.dailygood.org/story/2025/the-importance-of-quiet-time-alan-lightman/.

10. Josh Howarth, "Worldwide Date Social Media Usage (New 2024 Data)," Exploding Topics, May 10, 2024, https://explodingtopics.com/blog/social-media-usage#.

11. Williamson, Chris. 21 Truth Bombs to Radically Improve Your Life - Alex Hormozi (4K). YouTube, 29 Jan. 2024, https://www.youtube.com/watch?v=Gk8EGWoGnEQ&t=12s.

CHAPTER 9

1. Tracy, Brian. "How Self-Talk Determines Your Destiny." Entrepreneur, 4 Oct. 2017, https://www.entrepreneur.com/leadership/how-self-talk-determines-your-destiny/299293.

2. Goggins, David. Can't Hurt Me: Master Your Mind and Defy the Odds. Lioncrest Publishing, 2018.

3. "SHAOLIN MASTER | Shi Heng Yi 2023 - Full Interview With the MulliganBrothers." Mulligan Brothers Interviews, 4 Dec. 2023, www.youtube.com/watch?v=wGTo_hHVh-0.

4. Carmichael, Kenny. "The 4-Bucket Blueprint: Navigating and Mastering Life's Essential Domains." Medium, 18 Sept. 2023, www.medium.com/@kennycarmichael0708/the-4-bucket-

blueprint-4b6dfaf261e0.

5. Smilevida. "Whatever You Focus on Becomes Your Reality." Smilevida, 6 Jan. 2023, https://www.smilevida.com/post/whatever-you-focus-on-becomes-your-reality.

6. "Kevin Hart On Touring, Stand Up Comedy, Black Creatives, New Movies & More | Drink Champs." REVOLT, 24 Sept. 2022, www.youtube.com/watch?v=NjzbGcloyNY.

7. Goggins, David. Can't Hurt Me: Master Your Mind and Defy the Odds. Lioncrest Publishing, 2018.

8. Delony, John. The John Delony Show. Hosted by Dr. John Delony, Ramsey Network, www.ramseysolutions.com/shows/the-john-delony-show.

9. Robert Sapolski, *Why Zebras Don't Get Ulcers* (Holt Paperbacks; 3rd Edition, September 2004).

CHAPTER 10

1. Sharma, Robin. The Greatness Guide: One of the World's Most Successful Coaches Shares His Secrets for Personal and Business Mastery. Jaico Publishing House, 2006, p. 88. Available at https://www.azquotes.com/quote/1052296.

2. Band, Anthony. "Mindstorming Is the New Brainstorming." Medium, 1 Sept. 2023, https://medium.com/@anthonyband/mindsorming-is-the-new-brainstorming-3838f3df7392.

3. Robbins, Tony. "21 Empowering Leadership Quotes." Tony Robbins, https://www.tonyrobbins.com/tony-robbins-quotes/leadership-quotes.

4. Deepak Chopra, *Quantum Healing: Exploring the Frontiers of Mind/Body Medicine* (Bantam, May 1990).

5. Forest, Danny. "Becoming, Attracting and Creating, According to Buddha." The Startup, Medium, 12 Feb. 2018, https://medium.com/swlh/becoming-attracting-and-creating-according-to-buddha-49694643e5a.

6. Dr. Joe Dispenza, *Breaking the Habit of Being Yourself: How to Lose Your Mind and Create a New One*, (Hay House, LLC, January 2013).

7. Neil deGrasse Tyson, *Cosmic Queries: StarTalk's Guide to Who We Are, How We Got Here, and Where We're Going*, (National Geographic, 2021).

CHAPTER 11

1. Legge, Matthew. "Victimhood Is Tearing Us Apart: Here's What the Evidence Says About the Impact of Feeling Like a Victim." Psychology Today, 10 Feb. 2022, www.psychologytoday.com/us/blog/are-we-done-fighting/202202/victimhood-is-tearing-us-apart.

2. Legge, Matthew. "Victimhood Is Tearing Us Apart: Here's What the Evidence Says About the Impact of Feeling Like a Victim." Psychology Today, 10 Feb. 2022, www.psychologytoday.com/us/blog/are-we-done-fighting/202202/victimhood-is-tearing-us-apart.

3. Dr. Joe Dispanza, *You Are the Placebo: Making Your Mind Matter* (Hay House, 2014).

4. Dr. Joe Dispanza, *You Are the Placebo: Making Your Mind Matter* (Hay House, 2014).

5. FULL SEND PODCAST. "Kamaru Usman Says Canelo and GSP Are Scared to Fight Him!" YouTube, 24 Nov. 2021, https://www.youtube.com/watch?v=HZ2IhMRoOiQ.

6. "Deepak Chopra: The 5 Simple Steps That Will Make Your Mind Limitless!" |E241. The Diary of a CEO, 24 Apr. 2023, www.youtube.com/watch?v=t_pZ2D_nlDo.

7. Sam M. "Never Complain, Never Explain." Meditations on Stoicism, 13 Nov. 2022, https://medium.com/meditations-on-stoicism/never-complain-never-explain-c95boed3ea5c.

8. Aurelius, Marcus. Meditations. Translated by Gregory Hays, Modern Library, 2002, Book 8, Section 9.

9. Jay Shetty, *Think Like a Mink: Train Your Mind for Peace and Purpose Every Day* (Thorsons, 2020).

10. Williamson, Chris. Modern Wisdom. Hosted by Chris Williamson, www.chriswillx.com/podcast.

11. "19 Harsh Truths About Human Nature - Alex Hormozi." Chris Williamson, 3 Apr. 2023, www.youtube.com/watch?v=JuNOFW-oVn8&t=1s.

12. "Zack Tyree-Boise State University

Spring 2023 Commencement Speech."
Zack Tyree, 10 Dec. 2023, www.
youtube.com/watch?v=zC63LUOyUcc.

13. *Rocky VI* directed by Sylvester Stallone,
distributed by Metro-Goldwyn-Mayer
(2006).

14. "Jimmy Carr - The Secret Hacks For
Living A Fulfilled Life (4K)." Chris
Williamson, 9 Oct. 2023, www.
youtube.com/watch?v=ms02ezkAcYw.

15. Thomas, Eric. "What Are You Doing?
Wake Up! It's Showtime! Let's Go!"
Facebook, 2023, https://www.facebook.
com/reel/883406516897711.

16. Tyrese Gibson, *How to Get Out
of Your Own Way* (Grand Central
Publishing, reprint ed. 2002).

17. "Jay Shetty: The 3 Simple Things A
Happy Life Needs | E119." The Diary
of a CEO, 14 Feb. 2022, www.youtube.
com/watch?v=nYrjhv-AFZA&t=5410s.

18. "Manifest ABUNDANCE: 5 Limiting
Beliefs Blocking Your QUANTUM
Breakthrough | Price Pritchett." Lewis
Howes, 20 Sept. 2023, www.youtube.
com/watch?v=JCbSVBlCAIc.

19. Waitley, Denis. The Psychology of
Winning: Ten Qualities of a Total
Winner. Berkley Publishing Group,
1986.

20. Donald Miller, *Scary Close: Dropping
the Act and Finding True Intimacy*
(Thomas Nelson/HarperCollins, 2014).

CHAPTER 12

1. Dr. Seuss, *The Lorax* (Random House
Books for Young Readers, 1971).

2. Milken Institute. (2016, May 3). End of
an era: A conversation with NBA great
Kobe Bryant. YouTube. https://www.
youtube.com/watch?v=5ma2oQfiLF4

3. Because We Care. "Jelly Roll's Wisdom:
The Windshield vs. Rearview Mirror
Perspective." Because We Care, 13
Nov. 2023, https://becausewecare.
com/2023/11/13/jelly-rolls-wisdom-
the-windshield-vs-rearview-mirror-
perspective/#:~:text=Jelly%20
Roll%E2%80%99s%20metaphor%20
encourages%20us%20to%20
prioritize%20what,open%20
ourselves%20to%20endless%20
possibilities%20and%20new%20hori.

4. Yalung, Brian. "'I Love It When

Everybody Thinks We're Kind of Down
and Out' – Kobe Bryant Was on a
Mission During the Lakers Struggles,
Months After Their Three-Peat." MSN
Sports, 28 Aug. 2024, www.msn.
com/en-us/sports/nba/i-love-it-when-
everybody-thinks-were-kind-of-down-
and-out-kobe-bryant-was-on-a-mission-
during-the-lakers-struggles-months-
after-their-three-peat/ar-AA1pAa42.

5. "Michael Jordan and Stephen Curry
Talk Ryder Cup, Golf, Basketball."
Stephen Curry, 26 Sept. 2021, www.
youtube.com/watch?v=ylqVudWf3fQ.

6. "How to Break the Addiction to
Negative Thoughts & Emotions in
31 Minutes | Trevor Moawad." Tom
Bilyeu, 3 Mar. 2020, www.youtube.
com/watch?v=5lCeWtXPKko.

7. "Dry Creek Wrangler (the 'Philosopher
Cowboy') - Dewayne Noel Ep #32."
The Chasing Mountains Podcast,
22 Nov. 2023, www.youtube.com/
watch?v=c-tbLb4O2Pk.

8. David Goggins, *You Can't Hurt Me:
Master Your Mind and Defy the Odds*
(Lioncrest Publishing, 2018).

9. Verschuren, Dennis. "Life's Hard
Knocks: How Adversities Reshape Our
Brain's Future." Neuroscience News,
Radboud University, 21 Aug. 2023,
www.neurosciencenews.com/adversity-
brain-neuroscience-23789/.

10. Cohen, Sandy. "Training the Brain to
Reconsider Troubling Thoughts Can
Ease Mental Health Challenges, Says
UCLA Health Research Psychiatrist."
UCLA Health, 9 May 2023, www.
uclahealth.org/news/article/training-
brain-reconsider-troubling-thoughts-
can-ease-mental.

11. Bergland, Christopher. "More Proof
That Aerobic Exercise Can Make Your
Brain Bigger." Psychology Today, 8 Feb.
2016, www.psychologytoday.com/us/
blog/the-athletes-way/201602/more-
proof-aerobic-exercise-can-make-your-
brain-bigger.

CHAPTER 13

1. Quotes Guide. "You Don't Have to Be
Great to Start, but You Have to Start to
Be Great – Zig Ziglar." Quotes Guide,
https://quotes.guide/zig-ziglar/quote/

you-dont-have-to-be-great-to-start-but-you-have-to-start-to-be-great/.

2. World Golf Hall of Fame. "Tiger Woods: World Golf Hall of Fame Acceptance Speech (2022 Induction)." *YouTube*, 9 Mar. 2022, https://www.youtube.com/watch?v=ny8HK_FmU_g.

3. Misner, Ivan. "Episode 461: The 7 Things I Learned from Starting a Business (Classic Podcast)." BNI Podcast, 15 June 2016, www.bnipodcast.com/2016/06/15/episode-461-7-things-learned-starting-business-classic-podcast/.

4. "Kevin Hart: Million Dollaz Worth of Game Episode 192." Million Dollaz Worth of Game, 7 Nov. 2022, www.youtube.com/watch?v=W6Hiv9Glw9E.

5. Keeping It 💯 @EarnYourLeisure #Investfest." The Official Steve Harvey, 7 Aug. 2022, www.youtube.com/watch.

6. Tracy, Brian. "Eat That Frog, Explained by Brian Tracy." Brian Tracy International, www.briantracy.com/blog/time-management/the-truth-about-frogs/.

7. Tracy, Brian. "How to Set Priorities Using the ABCDE Method." Brian Tracy International, www.briantracy.com/blog/time-management/the-abcde-list-technique-for-setting-priorities/.

8. "Douglas MacArthur Quotes." BrainyQuote.com. BrainyMedia Inc, 2025. 24 January 2025. https://www.brainyquote.com/quotes/douglas_macarthur_141016

9. Keller, Helen. "Life is either a daring adventure or nothing. Security does not exist in nature, nor do the children of men as a whole experience it. Avoiding danger is no safer in the long run than exposure." Goodreads, www.goodreads.com/quotes/526067-life-is-either-a-daring-adventure-or-nothing-security-does.

10. "Steve Jobs on Failure." Silicon Valley Historical Association, 31 Oct. 2011, www.youtube.com/watch?v=zkTfoLmDqKI.

11. Senra, David. "Kobe Bryant." David's Notes, 27 Jan. 2020, https://davidsnotes.substack.com/p/kobe-bryant

12. Williamson, Chris. "23 Harsh Truths Nobody Wants to Admit - Alex Hormozi (4K)." YouTube, 21 Aug. 2023, https://www.youtube.com/watch?v=M4PzOjM5BJQ&t=923s.

13. "Dale Carnegie Quotes." BrainyQuote.com. BrainyMedia Inc, 2025. 27 January 2025. https://www.brainyquote.com/quotes/dale_carnegie_132157

CHAPTER 14

1. Gasparovic, Justin. "55 Tim Grover Quotes About Unlocking Your Greatness." The Enemy of Average, 26 Nov. 2022, https://theenemyofaverage.com/tim-grover-quotes/.

CHAPTER 15

1. "Benefits of Mentoring for Young People." Youth.gov, www.youth.gov/youth-topics/mentoring/benefits-mentoring-young-people.

2. Delgado, Jennifer. "Law of Reversed Effort: The More We Want Something, the More We Push It Away." Psychology Spot, n.d., https://psychology-spot.com/law-of-reversed-effort/.

3. Seneca, "There are more things likely to frighten us than there are to crush us; we suffer more in our imagination than in reality," Goodreads. https://www.goodreads.com/quotes/7441529-there-are-more-things-likely-to-frighten-us-than-there

4. George Eliot, "It's never too late to be what you might have been," Goodreads. https://www.goodreads.com/quotes/10546615-it-s-never-too-late-to-be-what-you-might-have

5. Marcus Aurelius, "Our life is what our thoughts make it," Goodreads. https://www.goodreads.com/quotes/27798-our-life-is-what-our-thoughts-make-it

6. Carl Jung, "Thinking is difficult, that's why most people judge," Goodreads. https://www.goodreads.com/quotes/657586-thinking-is-difficult-that-s-why-most-people-judge

7. Lao Tzu, "Care about what other people think and you will always be their prisoner," Goodreads. https://www.goodreads.com/quotes/80164-care-about-what-other-people-think-and-you-will-always

8. Pythagoras, "A fool is known by his speech, and a wise man by silence," Goodreads. https://www.goodreads.com/quotes/11666617-a-fool-is-known-by-his-speech-and-a-wise

9. Confucius, "If you are the smartest person in the room, then you are in the wrong room," Goodreads. https://www.goodreads.com/quotes/785494I-if-you-are-the-smartest-person-in-the-room-then

10. Rumi, "The quieter you become, the more you are able to hear," Goodreads. https://www.goodreads.com/quotes/6822193-the-quieter-you-become-the-more-you-are-able-to

11. Smile Because. "Life Is a Dance Meditation – from Alan Watts." Smile Because, 27 Sept. 2023, https://smilebecause.com/life-is-a-dance-meditation-from-alan-watts/.

12. Jones, Maya A. "Dave Chappelle Tells Allen University Audience You 'Gotta Keep Your Ethics Intact.'" Andscape, 21 Mar. 2017, https://andscape.com/features/dave-chappelle-tells-allen-university-audience-you-gotta-keep-your-ethics-intact/.

13. Williamson, Chris. Master Human Nature & Hack Your Way To Success - Steven Bartlett (4K). YouTube, 2 Oct. 2023, www.youtube.com/watch?v=JBgwF8aHByI&t=2448s.

14. "The First 20 Hours – How to Learn Anything | Josh Kaufman | TEDxCSU." TEDx Talks, 14 Mar. 2013, www.youtube.com/watch?v=5MgBikgcWnY.

15. "Benefits of Mentoring for Young People." Youth.gov, U.S. Department of Health and Human Services, https://youth.gov/youth-topics/mentoring/benefits-mentoring-young-people.

CHAPTER 16

1. "Joshua Bell's 'Stop and Hear the Music' Metro Experiment | The Washington Post." Washington Post, 11 Apr. 2007, www.youtube.com/watch?v=hnOPuo_YWhw.

2. Lieberman, Alex. "Why Surrounding Yourself with the Right People Is the Key to Success." Thrive Global, 16 May 2019, www.community.thriveglobal.com/why-surrounding-yourself-with-the-right-people-is-the-key-to-success/.

3. Oreskovic, Alexei. "The PayPal Mafia Still Rules Silicon Valley." Fortune, 21 July 2024, www.fortune.com/2024/07/21/paypal-mafia-silicon-valley-thiel-hoffman-botha-rabois-musk/.

4. Eker, T. Harv. Secrets of the Millionaire Mind: Mastering the Inner Game of Wealth. HarperCollins, 2005.

CHAPTER 17

1. "Alex Eubank - God Cured My Anxiety & Depression | EP. 23." George Janko, 15 June 2023, www.youtube.com/watch?v=tUaAZRKNBQA.

2. "Story: How Big Is God." Daily Ten Minutes, n.d., www.dailytenminutes.com/2018/09/story-how-big-is-god.html.

3. "Kirk Franklin Gives Moving Speech As He Wins Gospel/Inspirational Award | Soul Train Awards 19." Soul Train, 18 Nov. 2019, www.youtube.com/watch?v=9xO-ypr-RE8.

4. "God Never Removes Something from Our Lives Without Replacing It with Something Better." Elizabethton Star, 24 May 2022, 8:14 a.m., https://www.elizabethton.com/2022/05/24/god-never-removes-something-from-our-lives-without-replacing-it-with-something-better/.

5. "The Andrew Tate Interview - PART 1 | EP. 47." George Janko, 7 Dec. 2023, www.youtube.com/watch?v=gnZmRWTSyLs.

6. "The Andrew Tate Interview - PART 1 | EP. 47." George Janko, 7 Dec. 2023, www.

www.ingramcontent.com/pod-product-compliance
Lightning Source LLC
Chambersburg PA
CBHW042315120626
46547CB00022B/2077